A GARDENER'S GUIDE TO

Hedges, Lawns & Groundcover

Editor Richard Rosenfeld
Series Editor Graham Strong

MURDOCH BOOKS

Murdoch Books UK Ltd, Ferry House, 51–57 Lacy Road, Putney, London SW15 1PR

CONTENTS

*ABOVE: A wonderful swathe of rich purple is created by this
groundcover planting of erica.*

*LEFT: The fine edge of this formal lawn sets off the adjacent border
perfectly, contrasting with the rich colours of the roses.*

GROWING HEDGES

*Hedges have many uses, especially
as screens, fences and windbreaks.
In suburban areas they are most
often used to screen out ugly views,
create a sense of privacy or divide
off a utility area from the rest of
the garden. In formal garden designs,
low, clipped hedges are very popular
as edgings or they can be used to
create a parterre.*

In rural districts, dense prickly hedges of hawthorn
(*Crataegus* species), wild rose (*Rosa* species), firethorn
(*Pyracantha* species) and barberry (*Berberis* species) have
traditionally been used instead of fences as they keep
animals in and also provide shelter from wind. Hedges are
sometimes planted as noise barriers, but their effectiveness
varies considerably. However, even blocking out the sight
of the noise source can be helpful.

LEFT: The strong rectangular form of this clipped Camellia
sasanqua *hedge contrasts strongly with the mounded shapes of weeping
Japanese maples in front, and the fiery sugar maples in the background.*

NEATLY CLIPPED HEDGES and shaped plants, especially standards and topiary, are the essence of formal gardens. In the very stylish setting of this country garden, tightly pruned dwarf box hedges are planted in circles around rows of standard bay trees.

PLANT SELECTION

When selecting plants for screens and hedges, make sure the chosen species suits your local climate, as well as the aspect and soil of your garden. Consider, too, the height and spread of the plant. A vigorous, tall-growing shrub for a 2m- (6½ft-) high hedge can mean a lot of time and work are spent on training and pruning the hedge to shape.

Most hedges are long-term plantings – don't just opt for the fastest growing species. If quick screening is essential, consider planting fast-growing 'nurse' trees, such as wattle, behind your slower growing, long-term plants. They can be removed once the main hedge has developed some fullness.

Evergreen shrubs are best for screening, but do not rule out deciduous shrubs. They may be appropriate if you want winter sun in the screened part of the garden, and the mass of bare branches will still give some privacy.

Selection of plant species will also depend to a great extent on your primary reason for establishing a hedge. In suburban gardens you may want to create an outdoor living space by screening off neighbouring properties, or to conceal an ugly view, unsightly structure or utility area from the rest of the garden. Don't use a particularly prickly or thorny plant in these areas as children or adults could hurt themselves if they fell against them.

HEDGE PLANTS

FORMAL HEDGES

- box
- cherry laurel
- cypress
- dwarf honeysuckle
- firethorn
- holly
- lavender
- photinia
- privet
- *Camellia sasanqua*
- spindle bush

INFORMAL HEDGES

- abelia
- cotoneaster
- elaeagnus
- escallonia
- fuchsia
- laurustinus
- rose
- rosemary
- spindle tree
- wattle

If you grow a hedge to delineate the boundary of your property, make sure you know exactly where the boundary lies before you start, and whether you want a real barrier or just an indication of the fenceline.

A hedge may be grown as a windbreak, taking into account the fact that it filters the wind but doesn't increase wind speed on the lee side as can happen with solid structures. A hedge that is not too dense is best. There are plenty of variegated evergreens that look good in winter sun.

ESTABLISHING A HEDGE

Soil preparation

Before digging trenches or holes for planting, use a string line and pegs to mark the planting positions. This is essential for formal hedges to ensure straight lines and even spacing. It is less important for informal hedges but, even so, it will give a better finished appearance. Dig the planting trench, or holes for individual plants, and check the drainage by filling them with water. If there is water still lying in the base after about twenty-four hours, you may need to put in subsoil drains.

Because hedges are close-planted, root competition is intense and you must therefore dig in plenty of well-decayed manure or compost a month before planting. When it is time to plant, add scatterings of fish, blood and bone, which is a slow-release fertilizer, to the soil. It adds nitrogen (promoting vigorous plant growth) and phosphates (encouraging healthy root growth). It gives the hedge a head-start and helps it quickly to become established and happy in its position. Clay soil needs breaking up with horticultural grit.

A VARIEGATED PIERIS hedge borders this path, softening the effect of the dry-stone wall that runs along the other side.

Planting

Most hedge plants are placed from 50cm–1m (20in–3½ft) apart, depending on their growth habit and the hedge style. Very close planting tends to make plants grow taller as they compete for sunlight. Water the plants in their pots the night before, or at least a couple of hours before planting.

Having removed the plants from their pots, loosen the root ball, and plant so that the soil level is the same as it was in the pots. Give them a thorough watering, and then mulch the area with old manure or compost. Regular watering and mulching is essential. You can also plant bare root specimens between the months of November and March.

TYPES OF HEDGES

Formal or informal

Hedges may be formal or informal. Formal hedges can be used to good effect in gardens of any size and may cover a large or small area. They are usually made from plants with small leaves, as large leaves would be cut in half when the hedge is trimmed and result in an untidy appearance. Well-kept formal hedges can be very labour intensive when it comes to clipping. Unless you grow miles of hedge this should not be a problem. Tall clipped hedges can be a problem though, requiring ladders and boards to cut the uppermost parts.

Informal hedges, which do not have neat outlines, don't need as much attention as formal hedges and can usually be maintained with only one or two clippings a year. In fact, they may not need any clipping at all. Some informal hedges simply need the occasional removal of a wayward stem or branch. Informal hedges probably have a greater impact if they span a reasonably long distance. But remember that without clipping, hedges will grow quite wide and take up quite a bit of space.

SHRUBS FOR A MIXED HEDGE

SCREENING HEDGES

• box	• leyland cypress
• cotoneaster	• privet
• escallonia	• spindle bush
• holly	• yew

FLOWERING HEDGES

• fuchsia	• quickthorn
• hebe	• rhododendron
• honeysuckle	• rose
• lavender	• vibernum

HEDGES FOR BERRIES AND 'CATKINS'

• barberry	• ivy
• cotoneaster	• privet
• holly	• firethorn
• itea	• rose

Mixed hedges

For variety in a hedge you can use plants of a species that has flowers of different shades, for example camellias. However, the most striking effects come when you have continuity of both foliage and flower colour. Hedges or screens of mixed shrubs only look their best when they are quite long. They also look more harmonious if they grow to the same height.

For a mixed hedge you can choose plants that have a similar leaf texture and shape, or you can go for a complete contrast, although this is usually only an option for hedges of considerable length. Over a short distance the hedge may look spotty if you use more than two species.

Low-clipped hedges for garden borders are sometimes made up of two species such as lavender and box, or lavender and small-leaved honeysuckle, giving contrast of both colour and texture. This can be very effective as the small scale allows you to see the repeated pattern.

RIGHT: This hedge achieves an architectural quality as it divides the garden. It needs to be accurately sheared to maintain its form.

BELOW: This formal hedge of Japanese box encloses a rose garden. Striking primary colours always stand out best, like this bold red rose.

BELOW: The sinuous curves of this formal photinia hedge give an illusion of distance.

BELOW: In this elegant, formal garden, an urn planted with echeveria and surrounded by a circle of trimmed box forms a neat focal point.

ABOVE: Starkly contrasting colours are here used to great effect to create a sculptural feature and a backdrop for a seating area.

ABOVE: The dark, glossy foliage on this cherry laurel provides a foil for the brilliant autumn colour of deciduous trees.

ABOVE: Bamboo has been used here to make temporary screens while slow-growing hedges mature. It is decorative in its own right.

ABOVE: This pretty, informal hedge of Camellia sasanqua perfectly matches the relaxed sub-tropical style of the house and garden.

ABOVE: A photinia hedge with pinky-red new growth is here used in place of a fence.

BELOW: A tightly clipped spindle bush hedge divides a utility area from the garden.

ABOVE: Vertical pillars of cypress punctuate the squared blocks of a clipped conifer hedge in this very formal arrangement. The rounded shapes of the cypresses soften the geometric style.

PRUNING

Shaping

Opinions differ on how to go about training and pruning a hedge. Some gardeners believe the plants should be allowed to grow to the desired height before the leading growth is cut off. Tip pruning of the lateral branches is carried out as seems necessary. Once the leading shoots are taken out, lateral growth should increase. This method suits informal hedges.

To develop a dense formal hedge, it is better to severely cut the vertical growth as soon as the plants are established, to encourage low branching, and then to continue cutting all upward growing shoots until the base has filled in well.

Always prune your hedge so that the top is just slightly narrower than the bottom, to prevent the lower growth dying back through lack of sunlight (see the diagrams opposite). This is especially important with conifers such as cypresses because once the lower growth dies, it does not usually regenerate. Conifers should be pruned little and often, and never into older wood, as many of them have no dormant buds on their stems capable of reshooting from bare wood.

The right equipment

Most domestic hedges can be managed with hedging shears. If, however, you have very extensive hedges to maintain, it may be worth investing in power-driven mechanical shears. With electric sheers use a special circuit-breaker device that cuts out if the lead is cut or severed, and always wear goggles to prevent shards of wood flying in your eyes. If you have to mount a ladder to trim the top parts of a hedge, be certain that the ladder is firm and steady.

ELECTRIC HAND SHEARS make trimming this small-leaved honeysuckle hedge both quick and easy.

HAND CLIPPERS are used to shape, not shear this variegated pittosporum.

THIS LAURUSTINUS HEDGE is being trimmed with the aid of a string line. It ensures that the hedge is perfectly straight, something difficult to achieve by eye.

SHAPING A HEDGE

THE SLIGHTLY NARROWER top of this hedge prevents the lower growth from dying out and ensures fullness of foliage all over.

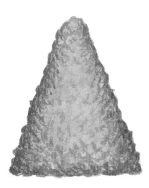

A PYRAMIDAL SHAPE is easiest to achieve if you start with a plant that has a natural taper to the top. Cypress and juniper are ideal.

A ROUNDED or bun shaped hedge may be difficult to maintain if it is too high or wide. You need to be able to prune across the top.

WHAT CAN GO WRONG?

Yellow leaves
• Plants may have been overwatered or they may be too dry.
• Plants may need feeding: fertilize them if this has not been done for two or three months and see if there is any improvement within the next two or three weeks.
• Older leaves on shrubs may turn bright yellow before dropping off. Don't worry, they have finished their useful life.

Curled or distorted leaves
• Look for aphids, small sticky insects clustering on the new growth. You can wash them off with a hose, spray them with soapy water or use an insecticidal soap or chemical spray.
• Some virus diseases manifest themselves this way and there is no cure for viruses in plants. Consult reference books or a nursery to see whether your plant is likely to have this problem.
• Check that there has been no drift of any herbicide from nearby spraying. Even very small amounts of spray drift can distort the leaves on those plants that are very sensitive to chemicals.

Black spots on leaves
• These may be fungal leaf spots. Avoid wetting the leaves when hosing and avoid watering plants late in the day.

Grey/white powder on leaf surfaces
• This deposit is probably powdery mildew, which affects a wide range of plants. Avoid watering gardens late in the day and spray plants with a chemical treatment if necessary.

Mottled leaves
• Mottling on leaves is usually associated with sap-sucking insects such as scales and thrips, and mites (which are not true insects). Plants that are under stress are more frequently attacked by these insects. Stress may be induced in plants by drought or overwatering, or simply by trying to grow a plant outside its preferred climate or aspect.
• Scales may be flat or rounded in various sizes and colours. Small infestations may be wiped off with a damp cloth. Control severe infestations by giving plants a chemical spray such as Malathion or insecticidal soap.
• Mites can be a particular problem in hot, dry weather. Hosing the foliage helps to reduce the numbers and may avoid the need for spraying. Note though that many mites are predators of insects or other mites, and are beneficial.

Holes in leaves or on leaf margins
• This may be snail or slug damage. Search for snails as they are often quite high up in the foliage and so do not take baits. Pick them off by hand. Keep a special watch at night. Baits can be used at the base of plants if you don't have pets.
• Caterpillars, weevil beetles and snails also eat leaves. You may need to dust your plants on several consecutive nights with derris dust, or spray the plants with carbaryl if damage persists. This is only likely in rare, extreme cases.

Sooty mould
• This dry, black coating on the leaf surface grows and feeds on sticky honeydew secreted by sap-sucking insects such as aphids and scales. The honeydew looks like tiny beads of sticky sweat. Once the insect pest is controlled, the sooty mould will gradually weather off. Hosing helps; large-leaved plants can be wiped with a damp cloth.

Sudden death of plant
• If the leaves have turned brown but remain attached to the plant, the plant has probably died of root rot. The root systems may have been damaged by excessive watering, from rain or irrigation, quite some time before the plant dies, especially in cold, wet winters. Make sure the soil is lightened for new, hardier plants. When stress such as an extremely hot or windy day is experienced, the damaged root system cannot cope and the plant appears to have died almost overnight.
• If a plant is suffering from drought the leaves may be brown and rapidly drop off when the plant is given a good watering. These plants may recover if they have not been water-stressed for too long.

CLIPPED BOX was used to create this wonderful modern version of a parterre garden. A topiary peacock has pride of place in the centre, while the low hedges are interrupted by the formal pyramid and ball shapes. A parterre garden need not be large: the effect is achieved by the intricate shapes.

PARTERRE GARDENS

Parterre means 'on or over the ground' but it has come to mean a level space containing ornamental garden beds. Early parterre gardens were arranged in geometric patterns within an outer square. Flowers were not used as they distracted the viewer from the design, which was more important than the plants. A very limited range of plants was used.

In the later medieval period knot gardens were developed, and they evolved further during the early Renaissance period in Europe. The gardens were designed to be looked on from above, either from an upper floor of a building or from a garden terrace. Sometimes the pattern was punctuated with tightly clipped, formally shaped conifers. Often the ordered, formal parterre was used to offer a distinct contrast with the wider, natural landscape viewed in the distance. Gravel and brick dust were used on the ground between the clipped plants to further emphasize the design.

The formal parterre layout was incorporated into the grand gardens of Rome and Tuscany during the 15th and 16th centuries, and persisted in Italy until the end of the 18th century. These Italian gardens maintained a strict economy of plant material, with no distracting colour. By the middle of the 17th century in France, broderies or parterres were all the rage. Broderies were made using the elaborate patterns, colours and designs of the embroidered silks which were imported from India and China. The French fashion spread throughout Europe. Armies of gardeners were employed to maintain these floral artworks in perfect condition. Although many of these famous gardens have been destroyed and are known only from engravings and paintings, some have been restored and can still be seen.

Modern parterre gardens

Today there is a revival of interest in parterre gardens. Modern interpretations are more flexible than their historical ancestors and may have informal plantings inside a formal shape that is defined by small hedges. These hedges are often planted with English or Japanese box. The dwarf edging box, *Buxus sempervirens* 'Suffruticosa', is most commonly used and while there are other forms of box this is the one for small topiary. Other modern parterre gardens are created with strict geometric designs and use a limited range of plants with contrasting colour and foliage characteristics. Plants commonly used include box, cotton lavender, true lavender and small-leaved honeysuckle (*Lonicera nitida*).

If you want to have informal plantings inside a formal hedge, consider how much attention the plantings will need and whether they will look attractive for many months without intense management. Also, when planning the garden, remember that if the area is close-planted you will need to be able to reach into the centre of the planting from the side as there will be nowhere to step. And give some thought to whether a parterre garden suits the style of your house and whether you have the time or interest to devote to its maintenance. Such schemes invariably look best where the buildings can provide architectural formality and where they have loving owners willing to put in the hours.

TOPIARY

Topiary is the art of training and pruning plants into specific shapes. Many topiary shapes are geometric, with triangles or pyramids, cones and squares being widely used. Balls and cylinders are other very popular shapes, but plants can also be trained to resemble animals and birds or even architectural features. Peacocks and wrens have always been popular.

Topiary is an ancient art. It was practised by the Romans and spread throughout the Roman Empire as far as Spain and Turkey. Topiary was widely used in Italian and French gardens during the Renaissance and has been used in a great many gardens in Britain. Levens Hall in Cumbria is judged to be the finest surviving topiary garden in the world. It was originally developed in the 17th century, the hard-clipped shapes being composed of yew and box. Some of these shapes have become massive with time despite the regular shearing.

Topiary today

Topiary is once again becoming popular, one of the most commonly seen forms being a clipped, rounded ball. Plants are also trained into spirals, juniper being one of the most widely used plants for this form, and into layers of foliage with bare stem or trunk in between. These formally shaped plants are often used as large potted specimens to flank an entrance way. They have a place as accent plants to highlight a section of a garden or to draw the eye to a specific point.

A wider variety of plants is used today but still the most popular are the plants with fine, dense foliage such as juniper and cypress, and small-leaved evergreens such as box, privet and small-leaved honeysuckle.

Creating topiary

The creation of good topiary effects requires a great deal of time, patience and skill. Careful, painstaking clipping has to be done throughout the growing season. This input of time and skill is reflected in the high price charged for a good specimen at the nursery.

If you decide to try creating topiary for yourself, choose a young plant that is in vigorous growth. When you need to remove foliage right back to the trunk or stem, young plants will heal their scars less noticeably than older plants. Sometimes unwanted foliage can be rubbed off with the fingers, especially if it is young regrowth from a previous cut. And don't aim too high at your first attempt – start with a simple shape such as a ball, cube or pyramid.

First you will need to shape with secateurs, but once the plant begins to take on the form you want, growth can be shorn off quickly, little and often, using a pair of shears.

For your first efforts in topiary, it is best to select a plant that is vaguely the shape you want to achieve. If you would like a triangular or pyramidal shape, look for a plant that is wide at the base and has a natural taper towards its top. For rounded or ball shapes, choose a multi-stemmed shrub that has a good overall cover of foliage.

Don't make your first shaping too severe as you need to see how quickly new growth emerges from the pruned stems. If you are adventurous enough to try a layered look straight away you will need to select a tree or shrub specimen that has foliage almost to soil level, and one that is at least 1m (3½ft) high. Otherwise you won't have enough to work with.

Quick 'topiary'

Sometimes small-leaved plants and climbers are trained over wire shapes to create a particular form, and while this is a much quicker way to produce a finished specimen, it is not strictly speaking topiary. However, they do create a pleasing effect and are relatively maintenance-free. Some public parks, zoos and even railway stations have emblems and animals created this way – the finished product always creates interest with children and adults alike.

IN THIS LOVELY GARDEN a formal hedge of Japanese box encloses an informal planting of azalea, roses and lilac.

STANDARD BOX TREES on short stems accent the corners of this bed, with its tiny box hedges and massed mondo grass.

A YOUNG PLANTING of dwarf box is here laid out to complement the tall standard box trees. Some people call them 'lollipop' trees.

ABELIA X GRANDIFLORA
Abelia

SPLASHED WITH pale gold, the leaves of Abelia *'Francis Mason' can light up your garden. Plant it near darker plants for contrast.*

IF NOT TRIMMED too severely, abelia makes a dense and pretty hedging or screening plant. It is very easy to care for.

FEATURES

Informal

This evergreen shrub with slightly arching canes makes an easy-care informal hedge or screen. Growing to about 2m (6½ft) high and wide, it has glossy green leaves and produces masses of pink flowers throughout summer and into early autumn. Its decorative effect is prolonged by the persistent pinky-red calyces (flower bases) which remain on the bush until autumn. This is a long-lived plant. There is a variegated leaf form known as 'Francis Mason', which is generally less vigorous in growth.

CONDITIONS

Aspect
Grows best in full sun but tolerates some shade for part of the day. Since it isn't fully hardy, provide a warm, protected spot. These plants are best grown in city gardens that do not get blitzed by frosts.

Site
Needs well-drained soil, preferably enriched with organic matter, although it will grow in poorer soils.

ABELIA AT A GLANCE

Abelia x *grandiflora* is a fine evergreen shrub with dark glossy leaves and gently scented white flowers. Hardy to –5°C (23°F).

		RECOMMENDED VARIETIES
JAN	foliage 🌿	*Abelia chinensis*
FEB	foliage 🌿	A. 'Edward Goucher'
MAR	foliage 🌿	*A. floribunda*
APRIL	foliage 🌿	A. x *grandiflora*
MAY	foliage 🌿	A. x *g.* 'Francis Mason'
JUNE	foliage 🌿	A. x *g.* 'Goldsport'
JULY	flowering ✾	*Abelia triflora*
AUG	flowering ✾	
SEPT	flowering ✾	
OCT	foliage 🌿	
NOV	foliage 🌿	
DEC	foliage 🌿	

GROWING METHOD

Propagation
Grow abelia from semi-hardwood cuttings taken in late summer to early autumn, or from hardwood cuttings of leafless canes taken during the winter months. This is a remarkably unfussy plant.

Spacing
Set plants at about 1m (3½ft) intervals.

Feeding
Apply complete plant food in spring and again in midsummer.

Problems
No problems are known.

FLOWERING

Season
There is a long flowering period through summer and sometimes into autumn. Afterwards, the red calyces of the flower will often remain on the shrub, giving colour until the autumn.

PRUNING

General
The main pruning should be done in early spring. As an informal hedge it does not need shearing, which would spoil the arching habit of the growth. *Abelia triflora* is the tallest, reaching about 3m (10ft) high. It can be rather gaunt though. The best looking hedge plant is *Abelia* x *grandiflora* which is slightly shorter.

ACACIA
Wattle

A CREAMY YELLOW WATTLE in full bloom is a magnificent sight, and many have the added advantage that they bloom in winter.

ACACIA BINERVIA is one wattle that makes a fine hedge: it responds well to pruning, although it may never bloom.

FEATURES

Informal

Acacias are quite tender, best grown in sheltered gardens in the warm south-west, where they escape the frosts. They can be used as novel, mainly evergreen hedges about 2.1m (7ft) high. They provide marvellous soft delicate foliage and fluffy flowers, usually yellow, in early spring. The flowers appear on last year's wood. The best kinds for a hedge are *Acacia cultriformis*, and *A. verticillata*, known as prickly Moses. Both are natives of Australia. They need to be well pruned after flowering to promote an abundance of short stems creating a thick, bushy effect. In colder regions acacias are best grown against warm sheltered walls where they will not get blitzed by icy winds.

ACACIA AT A GLANCE

Acacias make a highly attractive, unusual, yellow-flowering hedge in warm-climate gardens. Hardy to 0°C (32°F).

		COMPANION PLANTS
JAN	foliage 🍂	Crocus
FEB	foliage 🍂	Daffodil
MAR	flowering ❀	Erythronium
APRIL	foliage 🍂	Fritillaria
MAY	foliage 🍂	Iris
JUNE	foliage 🍂	Scilla
JULY	foliage 🍂	Tulip
AUG	foliage 🍂	
SEPT	foliage 🍂	
OCT	foliage 🍂	
NOV	foliage 🍂	
DEC	foliage 🍂	

CONDITIONS

Aspect Most acacias prefer full sun for best results. Some, such as *Acacia binervia* and *A. longifolia* will tolerate exposed coastal conditions.

Site The soil must be well drained, but need not be particularly rich. Acacias will tolerate sites with slightly acid soils.

GROWING METHOD

Propagation Grow from seed removed from ripe pods. Pour almost boiling water over the seed and allow it to soak overnight before planting. Alternatively take semi-ripe cuttings in the summer.

Spacing Plant at 1–1.5m (3½–5ft) intervals.

Feeding Fertilizing is not essential. A light application of blood and bone may be given in spring.

Problems In the open acacias are remarkably trouble-free, assuming that frosts do not get them. Under glass, however, they are prone to red spider mites.

FLOWERING

Season Depends on the species chosen. Most flower in early spring. The milder the winter has been the better the flowers.

PRUNING

General For a formal shape, pruning may be necessary two or three times during the growing season but then you may get little or no flowering.

BERBERIS THUNBERGII
Barberry

AN UNPRUNED BARBERRY has a loose, open habit. Full sun is needed to maintain the colour of the burgundy and pink forms.

CLOSELY CUT barberry forms a living fence on this property. The trees behind provide lovely contrasts in foliage, shape and texture.

FEATURES

Formal or Informal

Growing about 1m (3ft) high and wide, this is a very spiny plant that makes a useful hedge where a real barrier is wanted. Although it is deciduous, growth is very dense. In the species, leaves are deep green but there are cultivars with foliage that is burgundy or burgundy splashed with pink. This shrub gives year-round value, producing small, bright yellow flowers in spring, followed in autumn by bright red berries that persist through winter. The foliage colours well before falling.

CONDITIONS

Aspect   Prefers full sun all day, though many happily tolerate part shade, or shade for some of the day.

BERBERIS AT A GLANCE

Deciduous *Berberis thunbergii* has good autumn orange-red colours, and makes an ornamental summer hedge. Hardy to −18°C (0°F).

JAN	/	RECOMMENDED VARIETIES
FEB	/	*Berberis darwinii*
MAR	/	*B. d.* 'Flame'
APR	flowering ✤	*B. dictyophylla*
MAY	flowering ✤	*B.* 'Goldilocks'
JUN	foliage ✿	*B.* 'Red Jewel'
JULY	foliage ✿	*B.* x *stenophylla*
AUG	foliage ✿	*B. thunbergii atropurpurea*
SEP	foliage ✿	*B. wilsoniae*
OCT	foliage ✿	
NOV	/	
DEC	/	

Site   Although barberry is tolerant of a range of soil types, this shrub will give its best growth in well-drained soils that contain plenty of organic matter.

GROWING METHOD

Propagation   The species can be grown from seed that is taken from ripe berries, cleaned and planted. Cultivars are best grown from semi-ripe cuttings taken in the summer.

Spacing   Barberry needs planting at about 50cm (20in) intervals for hedging.

Feeding   Apply complete plant food as soon as growth begins in spring. A thick spring layer of well-rotted organic matter will act as a mulch, keeping in moisture and feeding the soil.

Problems   Barberry is sometimes attacked by scale insects, which are readily controlled by spraying with insecticidal soap. In general though, these plants suffer from few problems, and they tend to look after themselves.

FLOWERING

Season   Bright yellow flowers appear in spring.

Berries   Flowers are followed by berries that ripen to bright red by autumn. They may persist during the early winter months.

PRUNING

General   The main pruning should be done in late winter but tip pruning can be done at almost any time. Thin each year by removing some growth down near the base.

BUXUS
Box

NEAT, GLOSSY FOLIAGE *characterizes common box, which is probably the most widely used of all hedging plants.*

THE PALE NEW GROWTH *on this Japanese box will darken as it ages. The compact rosettes of echeveria emphasise the formal hedge shape.*

FEATURES

Formal

Formal box hedges have been used for many centuries in Europe and are still used in many parts of the world. Box plants are very long lived. If left untrimmed, they can grow quite tall but for hedging are usually kept under 1m (3ft) high. There are several varieties in use for hedges. Common box (*B. sempervirens*) has very dark green, pointed leaves, while Japanese box (*B. microphylla* var. *japonica*) has lighter green, more rounded leaves. There is also a dwarf edging box (*B. sempervirens* 'Suffruticosa') with very small leaves and a compact habit which can be planted at 15cm (6in) intervals. Box plants need clipping only once or twice a year. Start gently pruning box at a young age to make sure that the plants bush out from low down and create a dense solid shape. Otherwise they can take on a sparse look.

BUXUS AT A GLANCE

Box is a first-rate hedging plant, giving well-defined, evergreen, topiarized shapes. Clip regularly. Hardy to –15°C (5°F).

JAN	foliage	
FEB	foliage	
MAR	foliage	
APRIL	flowering	
MAY	flowering	
JUNE	foliage	
JULY	foliage	
AUG	foliage	
SEPT	foliage	
OCT	foliage	
NOV	foliage	
DEC	foliage	

RECOMMENDED VARIETIES
Buxus sempervirens
B. s. 'Elegantissima'
B. s. 'Handsworthensis'
B. s. 'Latifolia Maculata'
B. s. 'Suffruticosa'
B. microphylla var. *japonica*

CONDITIONS

Aspect For dense compact growth, plants should be grown in full sun. They will tolerate partial even total shade.

Site Tolerant of poor soils, box does best in well-drained soil with plenty of decayed organic matter. Thrives on lime and chalk soils.

GROWING METHOD

Propagation From semi-ripe cuttings taken in summer.

Spacing For hedging box can be planted at 30–50cm (12–20in) spacings. While more informal hedges can be planted in zigzags, using two parallel lines, formal box hedges should be planted in straight lines.

Feeding Apply complete plant food in spring and again in midsummer. Give a February feed with nitrate of soda. It'll grow fuller and quicker.

Problems A virulent fungal box blight affecting *B. sempervirens* and its cultivars, as well as *B. microphylla* and *B. sinica* is spreading throughout the UK. Infected leaves turn brown and fall. Try to be sure to buy unifected plants. Prune and destroy any infected leaves.

FLOWERING

Season The tiny but lightly perfumed flowers appear during spring. They are very attractive to bees. Frequently pruned box may not flower.

PRUNING

General Formal box hedging should be pruned as often as needed to maintain its shape.

CAMELLIA SASANQUA
Camellia

THE CLEAR PINK FLOWERS *of* Camellia sasanqua *'Plantation Pink' are shown off to perfection by the rich glossy foliage.*

PRUNING *to a formal shape may reduce the quantity of blooms on this camellia hedge, but it will still look good throughout the year.*

FEATURES

Formal or Informal

Although other species of camellia can be grown as screening plants, *C. sasanqua* is the most suitable for use as hedges, whether formal or informal. Like all camellias, it is long lived. The growth habit of the cultivars varies and for hedging it is best to choose an upright grower such as 'Narumigata', 'Navajo', and 'Nodami-ushiro'. You can choose the height of your hedge but camellias are usually topped off somewhere between 2–3m (6½–10ft). Blooming in mid- to late autumn, the flowers may be single or double, and they come in a colour range of white, pale pink, rose, cerise and red.

CONDITIONS

Aspect   These camellias tolerate sun or shade but are probably best in shade for part of the day.

CAMELLIA AT A GLANCE

Camellia sasanqua is a terrific late-season flowering hedge, but is not suitable for the cold north with early frosts. Hardy to –15°C (5°F).

		RECOMMENDED VARIETIES
JAN	foliage	*Camellia japonica* 'Bob Hope'
FEB	foliage	*C. j.* 'Guilio Nuccio'
MAR	foliage	*C. j.* 'Kumasaka'
APRIL	foliage	*C. j.* 'Miss Universe'
MAY	foliage	*C.* 'Leonard Messel'
JUNE	foliage	*C. sasanqua* 'Narumigata'
JULY	foliage	*C. s.* 'Navajo'
AUG	foliage	*C. s.* 'Nodami-ushiro'.
SEPT	foliage	*C.* x *williamsii* 'Elsie Jury'
OCT	flowering	
NOV	flowering	
DEC	foliage	

They only withstand wall-to-wall sun when fully established, and even then their roots must be kept on the cool side. As a general rule, keep them sheltered from harsh cold winds which can quickly send them into a major sulk.

Site   Needs well-drained, slightly acid soil that has been heavily enriched with organic matter. Plants also need mulching with decayed manure or compost.

GROWING METHOD

Propagation   From semi-ripe cuttings taken in late summer.

Spacing   Plant at about 50cm (20in) intervals.

Feeding   Apply blood and bone fertilizer, or camellia and azalea food, when growth starts in spring and again in midsummer.

Problems   Root rot caused by overwatering or poorly drained soil will kill these plants, but otherwise they are fairly trouble free. In some years a fungal leaf gall has been known to occur on selected varieties, causing abnormal thickening and discoloration of new growth. Pick off and destroy any leaves that are affected by this pest.

FLOWERING

Season   There is a late flowering period which begins in the autumn.

Cutting   Flowers dismantle easily and so are not suitable for picking.

PRUNING

General   The main pruning should be done in late winter just before new growth begins. Trimming can be done at any time of the year.

CARPINUS BETULUS
Hornbeam

LINES OF DIFFERENT colour help this Carpinus betulus *to look quite at home, as well as creating a graceful corridor effect.*

ALTHOUGH IT DOES produce flowers in the spring, the vibrant leaves of C. betulus *make a wonderfully lush display of their own.*

FEATURES

Formal

The common hornbeam, *Carpinus betulus*, grows wild in many parts of Britain, mainly in the south-east, west, and up to Hereford. An extremely strong wood, it is used for butchers' chopping blocks. If left to grow it can form a massive tree, 18m (60ft) high. But it is also the mainstay of wild hedges, withstanding severe pruning, and is grown for its spring catkins and autumn colour when the leaves turn yellowish-orange. It is particularly useful on heavy ground, and is worth using if you have thick clay soil. It also makes a quick growing, traditional formal hedge, and is a good alternative to hawthorn, beech, holly, privet, laurel and yew. The form 'Aspleniifolia' has more shapely, toothed leaves. For a long hedge, seek a specialist supplier who sells inexpensive young plants in bulk.

CARPINUS AT A GLANCE

Ever-reliable deciduous hedging plant, looks best in a cottage garden. Spare plants can be used as background trees. Hardy to −18°C (0°F).

		COMPANION PLANTS
JAN	/	Bluebell
FEB	/	Crocus
MAR	/	Cyclamen
APRIL	foliage	Erythronium
MAY	foliage	Fritillaria
JUNE	foliage	Poppy
JULY	foliage	Primrose
AUG	foliage	Rose
SEPT	foliage	
OCT	foliage	
NOV	/	
DEC	/	

CONDITIONS

Aspect
Hornbeam thrives in full sun and partial shade. The lighter the position the more quickly and densely it grows.

Site
Gardeners on heavy clay soil need not worry too much. Extreme cases should be lightened, but it is not necessary to spend hours trying to provide impeccable drainage by adding copious amounts of horticultural sand and grit.

GROWING METHOD

Propagation
Take fresh cuttings in early summer.

Spacing
Set plants about 90cm (3ft) apart, depending on the density required.

Feeding
Hornbeam does not require over-rich, well-worked soil. Moderate fertility is quite acceptable. On planting add plenty of well-rotted organic matter, and mulch to keep in moisture. It should get off to a very good start.

Problems
Highly robust trees that take care of themselves. Need little fussing.

FLOWERING

Season
The big decorative feature is a massed display of catkins (yellow when male, and greenish when female) in the spring. Useful in cut-flower displays.

PRUNING

General
One of the principal advantages of growing hornbeam is that you can cut it back quite severely and it will always re-shoot, putting on plenty of new growth.

CHAENOMELES SPECIOSA
Japonica

THE DELICATE APPEARANCE *of the flowers belies the tough nature of japonica. Flowers can be apricot, white, pink or crimson.*

DENSE, TWIGGY GROWTH *and ease of cultivation make japonica a practical and secure choice for boundary planting.*

FEATURES

Informal

Also known as flowering quince, japonica is a deciduous, multi-stemmed shrub that grows 1.8–2.5m (6–8ft) high. The stems are thorny, making it good for barrier planting. Fairly quick growing, it is also long lived. Japonica is a great asset to the garden in winter, producing its flowers on the bare branches in the spring. There are several lovely cultivars with flowers in scarlet, apricot, crimson, pink or white. Examples can be closely planted and trimmed, but japonica looks unnatural when cut into a box shape. It is usually best to let japonicas grow naturally.

CONDITIONS

Aspect   Prefers full sun but can get by with just half a day of sun. Not happy in shaded areas.

CHAENOMELES AT A GLANCE

An excellent large deciduous shrub with beautiful scarlet flowers in the spring. Makes a good tapestry hedge. Hardy to –18°C (0°F).

		RECOMMENDED VARIETIES
JAN	/	*Chaenomeles* x *californica*
FEB	/	'Enchantress'
MAR	/	*C. japonica*
APRIL	flowering ❁	*C. speciosa*
MAY	flowering ❁	*C. s.* 'Moerloosei'
JUNE	foliage	*C. s.* 'Simonii'
JULY	foliage	*C. s.* 'Umbilicata'
AUG	foliage	*C.* x *superba* 'Crimson and
SEPT	foliage	Gold'
OCT	foliage	*C.* x *superba* 'Knap Hill
NOV	/	Scarlet'
DEC	/	

Site   Tolerates a wide range of soils as long as the drainage is good.

GROWING METHOD

Propagation   Japonica is most easily grown from cuttings of dormant hardwood, but can also be grown from semi-ripe cuttings taken in the summer.

Spacing   For an informal hedge, japonicas will need 1m (3ft) spacings between them.

Feeding   Japonica can be grown without supplementary feeding, but if the soil is poor give complete plant food in the spring. In dryish areas a spring mulch of well-rotted manure will both keep moisture in, and improve the soil quality.

Problems   The shrub itself has no major problems but do keep a look out for possible canker, scale insects and aphids. Canker is the most troublesome. The bark becomes raised and splits, and it tends to ring right round the affected stem, and everything above starts to die. Cut back to healthy wood, and spray with an appropriate fungicide. Ready-made sprays are available at garden centres.

FLOWERING

Season   Flowers are produced on the bare branches in spring to early summer.

Cutting   Stems of japonica can be cut to make a lovely indoor decoration.

PRUNING

General   The main pruning should be done straight after flowering. As the plant becomes very congested, saw out some of the older canes at ground level to make way for younger wood.

COTONEASTER SIMONSII
Cotoneaster

THE INTENSE COLOURS of cotoneaster berries make these useful plants true stars of the garden in the autumn and early winter.

THE THICK, TWISTING habit of cotoneasters provides a dense mass of foliage and stem, making for an effective barrier.

FEATURES

Informal

Cotoneasters are highly underrated. Few people think past *Cotoneaster horizontalis* but there are about 320 kinds that you can buy from specialist nurseries. They range from tight, hard mounds as big as a large pumpkin, to giants. *C. simonsii* is an award-winning semi-evergreen (in warm areas) or deciduous shrub, upright in growth. The leaves redden in the autumn, and the berries are bright orange-red. It can get quite big, about 1.8m (6ft) high and wide, but can be pruned and kept shorter. As a hedge it is definitely for the wilder part of the garden. Like most cotoneasters, the big selling point is the major show of bright berries, some hanging on well in winter.

COTONEASTER AT A GLANCE

Cotoneaster simonsii is a high-performance berrying shrub with white summer flowers and orange-red fruit. Hardy to −18°C (0°F).

		RECOMMENDED VARIETIES
JAN	/	*Cotoneaster acutifolius*
FEB	/	*C. conspicuus*
MAR	/	*C. franchetii*
APRIL	/	*C.* 'Herbstfeuer'
MAY	/	*C. hupehensis*
JUNE	foliage 🌿	*C. marquandi*
JULY	flowering ✽	*C. nitidus*
AUG	foliage 🌿	*C. simonsii*
SEPT	foliage 🌿	*C. splendens*
OCT	foliage 🌿	*C. divaricatus* 'Valkenburg'
NOV	/	
DEC	/	

CONDITIONS

Aspect   Provide full sun, though partial shade is acceptable. The more sun, the more growth, the more berries.

Site   Cotoneasters tolerate most soils, except for the extremes of dry and wet. As a general rule though, do not overfeed, and make sure that there is good drainage.

GROWING METHOD

Propagation   The easiest method is by seed. Sow fresh seed and cover the soil surface with grit. Keep warm indoors, and then put in the refrigerator for six weeks, followed by more warmth. Or take cuttings in mid- and late summer.

Spacing   Set *C. simonsii* about 90cm (3ft) apart.

Feeding   Unless the soil was remarkably poor in quality to begin with, extra feeding will not be necessary. If feeding is needed, a slow-release spring fertilizer, such as blood, fish and bone mixture, will then suffice.

Problems   One drawback of these plants is that they can be afflicted by a wide range of problems. Look out for the cotoneaster webber moth which makes the foliage darken and dry up, and for signs of silk webbing. Cut away affected areas and spray with permethrin.

PRUNING

General   Most tolerate regular pruning. They also survive hard pruning, but it takes several years for the shrub to perform well again.

X CUPRESSOCYPARIS
Leyland Cypress

THIS MAGNIFICENT HEDGE of Leyland cypress will be hard to maintain without a movable platform and mechanical shears.

THIS FORMAL CYPRESS HEDGE provides privacy for the garden, at the same time softening the effect of the masonry wall.

FEATURES

Formal

One of the fastest growing of all conifers, x *Cupressocyparis leylandii* may grow as much as 1m (3ft) per year. Unpruned, it may easily reach 18m (60ft), but it is generally grown as a tall hedge plant 3–4m (10–13ft) high. This is probably the most widely used conifer for hedging in Britain. Plants should be lightly pruned on the sides to fill out the basal foliage before they are topped at the desired height. Foliage is quite feathery and medium to light green. Leyland cypress adapts to a wide range of climates and soils and is long lived. There are several cultivars available, of which 'Castlewellan' and 'Robinson's Gold' seem to be the most common. The former has wonderful plumes of yellow foliage, while the latter has bronze-yellow spring foliage, turning rich yellow and then pale green.

LEYLANDII AT A GLANCE

Highly impressive, fast growing conifers that make marvellous feathery hedges. Need to be pruned regularly. Hardy to −18°C (0°F).

		RECOMMENDED VARIETIES
JAN	foliage	x *Cupressocyparis leylandii*
FEB	foliage	x *C. l.* 'Castlewellan'
MAR	foliage	x *C. l.* 'Galway Gold'
APRIL	foliage	x *C. l.* 'Haggerston Grey'
MAY	foliage	x *C. l.* 'Harlequin'
JUNE	foliage	x *C. l.* 'Leighton Green'
JULY	foliage	x *C. l.* 'Naylor's Blue'
AUG	foliage	x *C. l.* 'Robinson's Gold'
SEPT	foliage	
OCT	foliage	
NOV	foliage	
DEC	foliage	

CONDITIONS

Aspect   Prefers full sun for dense foliage cover.
Site   Adaptable to a wide range of soil types but grows well in heavy, poorly drained clay soils.

GROWING METHOD

Propagation   Grow from semi-ripe cuttings or lateral shoots with a heel of older wood. Take cuttings from late summer to early autumn. They can be quite slow to root. If you need a long hedge, inexpensive young plants are available in bulk from specialist suppliers.

Spacing   Planting intervals should be 1–1.5m (3–5ft).

Feeding   Apply complete plant food as growth begins in spring. The root zone should be mulched with decayed manure or compost.

Problems   No particular problems, but x *C. leylandii* can be a nuisance. It can quickly make a hedge big enough to drive your neighbours mad. Slow growth down by trimming them twice a year, keeping them at say 1.8m (6ft).

FLOWERING

Season   Produces insignificant male and female cones.

PRUNING

General   Side growth should be tip pruned from the first year on. Once the desired height is reached, the plant should be topped. For a formal hedge give regular overall shearing, maybe two or three times a year in warm climates. Taper the sides of the hedge so that the top is narrower than the base.

CUPRESSUS
Cypress

THESE CYPRESSES are not so severely trimmed that they have lost their natural look. They provide a good measure of privacy.

REGULAR, LIGHT SHEARING is needed to maintain the strict geometric form of this hedge. Cypress is ideal for a formal hedge.

FEATURES

Formal or Informal

Cypresses look their best when they are allowed to grow to their normal shape and tree-like size. Some, such as the Bhutan cypress (*Cupressus torulosa*) and the Italian cypress (*C. sempervirens* 'Stricta'), are used as hedge boundaries and windbreaks on large properties. Left unpruned, they eventually grow to 10m (33ft) or more. They are moderately slow growing but very long lived. Cypresses can be hedged but trimming must start when they are young, as there will be no regrowth from cuts made into older wood. If you want a small, shapely hedge, cypresses are not for you. They are for big gardens where big screens are required. For a good effect grow a range of different shaped conifers with different tones of green.

CONDITIONS

Aspect   Grow cypresses in full sun.
Site   Soil should be well drained but need not be

rich, although these trees respond well to soil enriched with organic matter.

GROWING METHOD

Propagation Cypress is best grown from semi-ripe tip cuttings taken in late summer. Species can also be grown from seed collected from ripe cones and stored in the refrigerator for four to six weeks before planting.

Spacing   Plant cypresses about 1m (3ft) apart.

Feeding   Apply in spring complete plant food to the soil below the outer edge of the foliage and then water it in well. Since large, tangled, mature conifers often make it impossible to get to the soil round the base, it is essential to give them a good start with a deep, wide planting hole crammed with well-rotted organic matter.

Problems   You might find seiridium canker a problem. This is signalled by yellow then dying foliage. Other symptoms of seiridium canker include the bark roughening up, and resin oozing from infected areas. The only course of action is to cut back affected growth; there is no chemical treatment. However, keeping the plants well watered and well fed will improve their vigour and reduce their vulnerability to disease.

FLOWERING

Season   Tiny male cones and larger female cones are a feature of this plant.

PRUNING

General   Stop trees when they have reached the desired height. Tip pruning the foliage will create dense growth, and make for an extremely compact barrier. Never cut into old wood or bare stems beyond the last spray of foliage.

CUPRESSUS AT A GLANCE

Marvellous evergreen conifers, often tall and stately, making solid tall hedges and windbreaks. Hardy to –18°C (0°F).

JAN	foliage	
FEB	foliage	**RECOMMENDED VARIETIES**
MAR	foliage	*Cupressus abramsiana*
APRIL	foliage	*C. bakeri*
MAY	foliage	*C. goveniana* var. *pygmaea*
JUNE	foliage	*C. macrocarpa*
JULY	foliage	*C. m.* 'Glauca Pendula'
AUG	foliage	*C. sempervirens*
SEPT	foliage	*C. s.* 'Stricta'
OCT	foliage	
NOV	foliage	
DEC	foliage	

ELAEAGNUS PUNGENS
Elaeagnus

WITH ITS ATTRACTIVE variegated yellow and green foliage, Elaeagnus pungens *'Maculata' makes a stylish hedge for any garden.*

THE PLANT THAT has it all. Elaeagnus pungens *provides year-round variegated foliage, sweetly scented autumn flowers and berries.*

FEATURES

Informal

For a foolproof, hardy, evergreen hedge, with a decent show of berries, elaeagnus comes in the very top league. *Elaeagnus pungens* grows about 1.8m (6ft) high and wide, and has small, white, sweetly scented autumn flowers hidden amongst the foliage, followed by fruit that quickly reddens. The shrub only requires minimal pruning to keep it in shape. There are other excellent forms. 'Dicksonii' is less vigorous but more upright, and has bright yellow-edged leaves, and 'Maculata' is a quick-growing, branching plant that has a big yellow patch in each leaf centre. The sunnier and hotter the summer, the better the show of berries. If you need an even bigger, denser hedge of elaeagnus, try *E. macrophylla*. The autumn flowers have a strong, sweet scent.

ELAEAGNUS AT A GLANCE

Elaeagnus pungens makes a terrific all-purpose hedge, offering shelter, colour and berries. Hardy to −18°C (0°F).

		RECOMMENDED VARIETIES
JAN	foliage ❀	*Elaeagnus pungens*
FEB	foliage ❀	*E. p.* 'Dicksonii'
MAR	foliage ❀	*E. p.* 'Frederici'
APRIL	foliage ❀	*E. p.* 'Goldrim'
MAY	foliage ❀	*E. p.* 'Maculata'
JUNE	foliage ❀	*E. p.* ' Variegata'
JULY	foliage ❀	
AUG	foliage ❀	
SEPT	foliage ❀	
OCT	flowering ✽	
NOV	flowering ✽	
DEC	foliage ❀	

CONDITIONS

Aspect — Though elaeagnus will grow in shade, they then tend to produce a disappointing show of autumn berries. The sunnier and hotter the conditions, the better.

Site — Not particularly fussy, any well-tended ground, avoiding extremes, is fine. Provide rich soil and good drainage.

GROWING METHOD

Propagation — Take semi-ripe cuttings in the summer. They quickly take. It is quite possible to raise elaeagnus from seed, but is hardly worth the bother given how relatively quick and successful are the cuttings.

Spacing — Set plants about 76cm (2½ft) apart.

Feeding — It is tempting with reliable performers like elaeagnus to plant them and leave them alone, but a regular spring mulch of well-rotted manure, or a feed of slow-release fertilizer, will ensure that the bold leaved variegated forms really develop well and stand out.

Problems — None of any note.

FLOWERING

Season — Though *E. pungens* does flower in the autumn, the display is not anything to get excited about. The eyecatching variegated foliage scores more points.

GENERAL

Pruning — Prune to maintain shape in the spring.

ESCALLONIA 'EDINENSIS'
Escallonia

BURSTING INTO BLOOM in late spring, Escallonia 'Edinensis' will keep producing interest through the summer and into autumn.

THE OVERALL distribution of flowers on this E. 'Edinensis' makes for a pleasing mixture of colour with the glossy green of the leaves.

FEATURES

Informal

Escallonia are underrated evergreen shrubs, with glossy leaves that in hot weather give off a gentle, sweet smell. The best kind to use for a hedge are the bushy ones that can be well clipped. 'Peach Blossom', growing 1.8m (6ft) high with pink flowers, and *Escallonia rubra* 'Crimson Spire' which is slightly taller with red flowers, are both impressive. The latter is traditionally grown in seaside gardens as a hedge windbreak, since the plants can withstand both wind and salt. 'Edinensis', with pinkish-red flowers in the first half of summer, grows about 2m (6ft) high. New flowering shoots keep appearing up until the autumn. Other forms of escallonia, like the white-flowering 'Iveyi', can be slightly more tender, and may need to be grown against warm sheltering walls in cold regions.

ESCALLONIA AT A GLANCE

Escallonia 'Edinensis' is a versatile shrub that makes a windbreak hedge, while giving a good show of flowers. Hardy to −15°C (5°F).

JAN	foliage ❀	RECOMMENDED VARIETIES
FEB	foliage ❀	*Escallonia* 'Edinensis'
MAR	foliage ❀	E. 'Peach Blossom'
APRIL	foliage ❀	E. *rubra* 'Crimson Spire'
MAY	flowering ❀	
JUNE	flowering ❀	COMPANION PLANTS
JULY	flowering ❀	Bluebell
AUG	flowering ❀	Daffodil
SEPT	flowering ❀	Fritillaria
OCT	foliage ❀	Hyacinth
NOV	foliage ❀	Tulip
DEC	foliage ❀	

CONDITIONS

Aspect   Keep out of the shade and give as much wall-to-wall sun as you can.

Site   Good drainage and decent, fertile soil are the key requirements. A well-tended garden, without extremes of soil type, will be fine.

GROWING METHOD

Propagation   The best method of propagation is to take cuttings during the summer. You can also do this over winter, but you will get quicker results with the former.

Spacing   *Escallonia* 'Edinensis' can eventually grow to about 2.4m (8ft) wide, but with pruning allow for a gap of 90cm (3ft).

Feeding   It is useful to keep up the soil fertility. Either mulch in the spring with well-rotted manure, or add spring helpings of slow-release fertilizer such as blood and bone.

Problems   Remarkably free of pests and diseases.

FLOWERING

Season   The main flowering burst lasts from late spring to midsummer, but extra flowers usually keep appearing through late summer and into the start of autumn.

PRUNING

General   Either prune after the main burst of flowering in midsummer, or if you want extra flowers leave it until the following spring. Overgrown, misshapen, tangled shrubs can be cut back hard without inflicting serious damage.

EUONYMUS FORTUNEI
Spindle tree

LOOKING AS IF it has been covered with a fine coating of snow, Euonymus fortunei 'Silver Queen' makes for a very elegant hedge.

THE OVERALL IMPRESSION of the E. fortunei is light and frothy, offering a pleasant contrast to shrubs with darker green foliage.

FEATURES

Informal

The species most usually grown as a hedge is *Euonymus japonicus*, but *E. fortunei* provides plenty of extra possibilities. It is usually regarded as semi-prostrate, but it is quite capable of bulking and mounding up, creating a substantial evergreen division. It is a slow grower, but eventually will look hugely impressive. It can be pruned and smartened up. Many gardeners grow it against walls or fences, where it actually starts to climb. 'Silver Queen' is the best known form, and it develops distinctive green leaves with a flashy white margin; in the cold it has a pinkish tinge. Other good forms include 'Emerald Gaiety' and the eyecatching 'Emerald'n'Gold', which turns reddish in winter. The more the shrub does mound up, the better it flowers and fruits, the latter being white.

EUONYMUS AT A GLANCE

Euonymus fortunei makes a fine division in large borders, or a sprawling kind of divider. Exceptional foliage. Hardy to −15°C (5°F).

JAN	foliage 🍂	COMPANION PLANTS
FEB	foliage 🍂	*Euonymus alatus*
MAR	foliage 🍂	*E. cornutus* var.
APRIL	foliage 🍂	*quinquecornutus*
MAY	flowering ❀	*E. europaeus* 'Red Cascade'
JUNE	foliage 🍂	*E. japonicus*
JULY	foliage 🍂	*E. latifolius*
AUG	foliage 🍂	*E. lucidus*
SEPT	foliage 🍂	*E. planipes*
OCT	foliage 🍂	
NOV	foliage 🍂	
DEC	foliage 🍂	

CONDITIONS

Aspect Full sun gives the best results. Light shade is acceptable, but otherwise keep away from the dark. Some wind protection helps. Cold and exposed positions do not often work well.

Site Average fertile soil is fine, with good drainage. A thick mulch of well-rotted organic matter in the spring, especially in hot dry sites, will work wonders.

GROWING METHOD

Propagation Take semi-ripe cuttings in the summer. For seed see *E. japonicus*.

Spacing Reckon on 1m (3ft) apart or more, but it depends what size shrubs you buy. If small, remember that they grow quite slowly. These shrubs do not sprint away.

Feeding Over-rich soil is not necessary. Average garden fertility is fine. A spring slow-release fertilizer is quite adequate.

Problems In general, euonymus is remarkably trouble free. In some locations powdery mildew may strike. Take appropriate chemical action and improve the growing conditions.

FLOWERING

Season A hot spring will produce greater flower growth, but you should get 10 days in May when it is thick with whiteish blossom.

PRUNING

General Gently prune in the spring, taking care not to try and create too formal a shape.

EUONYMUS JAPONICUS
Spindle bush

THE DENSE GROWTH and neat, rounded leaves of Euonymus japonicus *make for a compact habit that is ideal for hedging.*

A HEDGE of golden spindle bush, here pruned into a formal, compact block, forms a bright contrast to a low juniper hedge.

FEATURES

Formal

An evergreen shrub growing 3–4m (10–13ft) high and 2m (6½ft) or more wide in very old age, *Euonymus japonicus* can be hedged at any height over 1m (3ft). The species has glossy green leaves, but the many variegated cultivars with margins or splashes of cream or yellow are more common. A neat plant, *E. japonicus* is a moderate grower and long lived. It is a low-maintenance and adaptable shrub.

CONDITIONS

Aspect   Needs full sun for good, compact growth. Avoid the shade at all costs.

EUONYMUS AT A GLANCE

A good choice for a more traditional, well-shaped hedge with berries and bright leaves. Hardy to –5°C (23°F).

		RECOMMENDED VARIETIES
JAN	foliage ❧	*Euonymus japonicus*
FEB	foliage ❧	E. j. 'Albomarginatus'
MAR	foliage ❧	E. j. 'Aureus'
APRIL	foliage ❧	E. j. 'Macrophyllus'
MAY	flowering ❀	E. j. 'Macrophyllus
JUNE	foliage ❧	Aureovariegatus'
JULY	foliage ❧	E. j. 'Ovatus Aureus'
AUG	foliage ❧	
SEPT	foliage ❧	
OCT	foliage ❧	
NOV	foliage ❧	
DEC	foliage ❧	

Site   Soil should be well drained and preferably enriched with organic matter.

GROWING METHOD

Propagation   The species can be raised from cleaned seed extracted from berries in autumn and stored in the refrigerator to be sown in spring. Alternatively, cultivars can be grown from semi-ripe cuttings taken in the summer.

Spacing   Plant at about 1m (3ft), depending on how quickly you want the hedge to be established.

Feeding   Apply complete plant food in spring.

Problems   There are no known problems.

FLOWERING

Season   Greenish white flowers are produced in late spring but they are not a key feature of this plant in terms of its appearance.

Berries   Deep red berries follow the flowers in autumn. They score more points than the flowers.

PRUNING

General   Prune in the spring. The plant can also be trimmed at other times of the year to control any wayward growth. *E. japonicus* does not generally need a great deal of pruning. As with *E. fortunei*, make sure that you take care not to ruin the attractive leaves, one of the main reasons for growing this plant, especially the variegated forms like 'Ovatus Aureus'. It is therefore best to use secateurs.

FAGUS
Beech

THE TRANSLUCENT foliage of this forest beech can be harnessed to excellent effect as a hedge for the garden.

LATER IN THE SEASON the leaves of the common beech mature to a darker green, and the red-haired fruit appears.

FEATURES

Formal

It might be a tree, but it makes a terrific hedge from 1m–2.4m (3½–8ft) high. In the summer beech is thickly covered with fresh and then dark green leaves, many turning yellow-orange in the autumn before dropping. But many hang on to the tree, giving a thickish covering of beige-brown leaves. They add much needed colour in winter, and some screening. There are several beeches to choose from, but common beech (*Fagus sylvatica*), is the one traditionally grown. Seedlings easily take, and quickly bush out. A novel kind of beech hedge involves shearing all the branches off one side when it has fully grown, leaving leaves on top and down one side only. Looking through the leafy side when it is backlit by the sun is a very beautiful sight.

FAGUS AT A GLANCE

Excellent traditional hedging plant that can be well pruned giving a smart shape. Comes alive in the winter sun. Hardy to –15°C (5°F).

JAN	foliage 🍂	COMPANION PLANTS
FEB	foliage 🍂	Anemone
MAR	foliage 🍂	Bluebell
APRIL	foliage 🍂	Crocus
MAY	foliage 🍂	Daffodil
JUNE	foliage 🍂	Erythronium
JULY	foliage 🍂	Fritillaria
AUG	foliage 🍂	Hyacinth
SEPT	foliage 🍂	Iris
OCT	foliage 🍂	Scilla
NOV	foliage 🍂	Tulip
DEC	foliage 🍂	

CONDITIONS

Aspect The most successful results are achieved in the open where there is plenty of sunlight.

Site Rich, fertile soil is ideal, with good drainage. When digging planting holes, ideally over winter, add plenty of well-rotted organic matter, and some fish, blood and bone in the spring to give the young plants a good start. Avoid planting in thin soil like chalk that is relatively nutritionless .

GROWING METHOD

Propagation Raise by seed from late summer to autumn, or in late winter. It is much quicker though to buy inexpensive young seedlings; these fast-growing trees quickly take off. Since beech has shallow rooting, in open, windy sites it needs initially to be staked.

Spacing Set the plants about 45cm (18in) apart, within a guideline of 30–60cm (1–2ft).

Feeding As with most shrubs, provide a deep planting hole that has had plenty of well-rotted organic matter added. Heavy clays need to be broken up with plenty of horticultural sand and grit.

Problems Remarkably trouble free.

FLOWERING

Season Beech trees and hedges do have tiny flowers that develop into nuts with red, hairy shells. These can add to the overall charm of the beech, but the chief reason for growing beech is the leaf colour in a mixed tapestry hedge.

Pruning Prune from the end of autumn to the start of spring, to maintain shape and size.

FUCHSIA 'RICCARTONII'
Fuchsia

THE LONG-LASTING flowering season of Fuchsia *'Riccartonii' provides a blaze of colour throughout the summer and into autumn.*

DRIPPING WITH pendulous scarlet flowers, this F. *'Riccartonii' makes a wonderful contrast to the grey stone wall next to it.*

FEATURES

Informal

Fuchsias make excellent hedges. Travel around Ireland and you'll see them growing like this in quiet country lanes. *Fuchsia magellanica* tends to be used in this context. This can grow 2.4m (8ft) high and actually comes from South America where it is pollinated by hummingbirds. There are several hardy alternatives. *F.* 'Riccartonii' grows about 2m (6ft) high, with the same spread, and produces masses of small scarlet flowers. And if you need a slightly smaller, scarlet-flowering hedge, *F.* 'Mrs Popple' grows about 1.2m (4ft) high. Given the range of possible choices it is well worth visiting a specialist nursery. Do check that the plants are fully hardy though. Most need to be over-wintered indoors, while a few will survive outside, especially if protected in freezing spells under piles of bracken.

FUCHSIA AT A GLANCE

F. 'Riccartonii' makes a first-rate bright red flowering hedge, though like most fuchsias it is deciduous. Just about hardy to −15°C (5°F).

		COMPANION PLANTS
JAN	/	Asarina
FEB	/	Clematis
MAR	/	Ipomoea
APRIL	foliage ❀	Jasmine
MAY	foliage ❀	Rose
JUNE	flowering ❀	Solanum
JULY	flowering ❀	Tropaeolum
AUG	flowering ❀	
SEPT	flowering ❀	
OCT	/	
NOV	/	
DEC	/	

CONDITIONS

Aspect   Full sun for a good flowering show, or at least partial shade is required.

Site   Most garden soils are fine, avoiding extremes of dry and wet ground. A large planting hole with well-rotted organic matter will suffice.

GROWING METHOD

Propagation   Take softwood cuttings in late spring, or firmer ones in the summer. They will root quite quickly. One large plant will provide enough cuttings to make a long hedge.

Spacing   Leave about 1.2m (4ft) between each plant, allowing for the required density.

Feeding   Fuchsias are not that hungry feeders, but it is worth keeping up the soil fertility with spring applications of a slow-release fertilizer.

Problems   While fuchsias are theoretically prone to all kinds of bugs and moulds, in practice they are quite resilient. A well-grown, well-tended shrub will look after itself.

FLOWERING

Season   An excellent show of flowers right through the summer and into the autumn.

PRUNING

General   Either cut them right back in the spring when growth begins, making sure the hedge is reasonably open and not too high. Or simply give it a haircut, nipping back to strong buds to promote new growth. Straggly hedges can be cut back hard to promote new shoots.

ILEX AQUIFOLIUM
Holly

VARIEGATED HOLLY with a cream leaf margin provides a fine contrasting backdrop for this little garden statue.

DECORATIVE AND SECURE, this holly hedge makes a great wall substitute. The tall, pink-flowered shrub is English hawthorn.

FEATURES

Formal or Informal

Evergreen holly makes a hardy, long-lived hedge. The glossy green leaves are spiny in most varieties and there are many cultivars available, some with cream or gold variegated foliage. Male and female flowers are usually borne on separate plants, and a brilliant display of scarlet or orange berries follows on the female plants. Left unpruned, holly grows into a fairly large tree but it is often hedged at about 3m (10ft) high or less. It makes an extremely good windbreak hedge, and also tolerates air pollution.

CONDITIONS

Aspect   Prefers a sunny spot. Variegated kinds look best in sun, where the colours really stand out.

ILEX AT A GLANCE

Ilex aquifolium has many excellent forms making marvellous, dense, free-berrying hedges. Hardy to −18°C (0°F).

		RECOMMENDED VARIETIES
JAN	foliage ❧	*Ilex aquifolium*
FEB	foliage ❧	*I. aquifolium* 'Argentea
MAR	foliage ❧	Marginata'
APRIL	foliage ❧	*I. aquifolium* 'Ferox'
MAY	flowering ✽	*I. aquifolium* 'Golden Queen'
JUNE	flowering ✽	*I. aquifolium* 'Handsworth
JULY	foliage ❧	New Silver'
AUG	foliage ❧	*I. aquifolium* 'Silver Queen'
SEPT	foliage ❧	*I. cornuta* 'Burfordii'
OCT	foliage ❧	*I. crenata*
NOV	foliage ❧	
DEC	foliage ❧	

Site   These plants will need well-drained soil enriched with plenty of organic matter. Heavy clay soil must be broken up and lightened with horticultural sand and grit.

GROWING METHOD

Propagation   To grow large numbers of plants, clean and sow the ripened berries, but to maintain the purity of cultivars grow them from semi-ripe cuttings taken in the summer. Use a hormone rooting powder to increase the success rate.

Spacing   Plant at 1m (3ft) intervals for hedging.

Feeding   Apply complete plant food in early spring.

Problems   Holly has few problems but keep an eye out for aphids which can attack young shoots.

FLOWERING

Season   The small, creamy flowers are borne in late spring and early summer.

Berries   The flowers are followed by berries which ripen through autumn, hanging on through winter. Note that the form called 'Silver Queen' and 'Golden Queen' are actually male, and that the otherwise excellent, self-pollinating 'J. C. van Tol' does not actually make the best hedge.

PRUNING

General   Main pruning is done in late winter but wayward growth can be trimmed off at other times as well. To make a formal holly hedge you may need to prune two or three times during the growing season, depending on the vigour of the growth.

LAVANDULA
Lavender

THE UPRIGHT SPIKES *of French lavender provide interesting vertical lines above the rounded form of a mature lavender bush.*

UNCLIPPED LAVENDER BUSHES *make informal hedges beside a path, where fragrance will be released as passers-by brush against them.*

FEATURES

Formal or Informal

Most lavenders grow into rounded bushes about 1m (3ft) high and wide, but some dwarf forms grow only 30–40cm (12–16in) high. All lavenders are suitable for hedging as they respond well to regular clipping. The highly aromatic foliage is grey-green and flower spikes may be pale lavender to rich purple. Plant a lavender hedge to define a path or to outline a terrace – these are the places where passers-by will brush against them and release the fragrance. Lavender can also be planted to provide colour contrast in a formal garden.

CONDITIONS

Aspect   Needs full sun for good dense growth. Keep them well away from the shade.

Site   Needs an open, well-drained soil that need not be rich. Add lime to very acid soil before

planting lavender. Heavy wet soil needs to be vigorously broken up with plenty of horticultural sand and grit.

GROWING METHOD

Propagation   Grow from tip cuttings taken from spring until autumn, or from lateral cuttings with a heel of older wood in autumn or early winter. The success rate is usually quite high.

Spacing   For hedging, plant lavenders at 45–60cm (18–24in) intervals, dwarf forms at 30–40cm (12–16in) intervals.

Feeding   Needs little fertilizer. Apply pelleted poultry manure in spring as growth begins.

Problems   Overwatering or poorly drained soils will induce the rotting of roots. Also beware attacks of honey fungus. The stems die back, and the attack can either be swift and sudden or quite gradual, lasting a number of years. The only solution is to dig up the affected plants entirely, dig over the area, and replant with shrubs that better resist such attacks. They include choisya, pieris and pittosporum.

FLOWERING

Season   The main flowering season is in the height of the summer, adding fresh grey-green foliage and blue flowers to planting schemes.

Cutting   The flowers make wonderful posies and can also be dried. Regular clipping may reduce the flowering display.

PRUNING

General   Clip the shrub little and often to maintain dense growth. If necessary, hard prune in late winter, but not into old wood.

LAVANDULA AT A GLANCE

Marvellous, free-flowering, aromatic shrubs that quickly make impressive hedges; a good alternative to box. Hardy to –5°C (23°F).

JAN	foliage	
FEB	foliage	
MAR	foliage	
APRIL	foliage	
MAY	foliage	
JUNE	flowering	
JULY	flowering	
AUG	flowering	
SEPT	foliage	
OCT	foliage	
NOV	foliage	
DEC	foliage	

RECOMMENDED VARIETIES

Lavandula angustifolia
L. a. 'Hidcote'
L. a. 'Munstead'
L. a. 'Twickel Purple'
L. x *intermedia*
L. lanata
L. latifolia
L. stoechas

LIGUSTRUM OVALIFOLIUM
Golden privet

A FAVOURITE PLANT for hedging since Victorian times, golden privet needs very little care indeed.

PATCHES of the plain green species are starting to appear in this golden privet hedge. They may take over unless they are cut out early.

FEATURES

Formal

Many of the 50 species of privet have been grown in the past as hedges. This variety, *Ligustrum ovalifolium* 'Aureum', or golden privet, can grow to 4m (12ft) but is usually seen hedged to 1–2m (3–6¹/₂ft). Its foliage may be variegated dark green and gold but is often almost entirely yellow. This is a quick growing, hardy and easy-care plant, able to tolerate a wide range of conditions. It can be grown as a solid dividing hedge, or can be clipped and pruned to give all kinds of different shapes. The form 'Argenteum' has leaves with a white margin if the yellow seems a bit too brash.

LIGUSTRUM AT A GLANCE

Excellent, all-purpose, robust hedge with summer flowers that can be shaped and pruned. Hardy to –18°C (0°F).

JAN	foliage	RECOMMENDED VARIETIES
FEB	foliage	*Ligustrum japonicum*
MAR	foliage	*L. lucidum*
APRIL	foliage	*L. lucidum* 'Excelsum
MAY	foliage	Superbum'
JUNE	flowering	*L. obtusifolium*
JULY	foliage	*L. ovalifolium* 'Argenteum'
AUG	foliage	*L. ovalifolium* 'Aureum'
SEPT	foliage	*L. vulgare*
OCT	foliage	
NOV	foliage	
DEC	foliage	

CONDITIONS

Aspect Must have full sun all day for dense growth and to retain the golden colour.

Site Should be well drained but it does not need to be rich. Giving privet a spring feed of slow-release fertilizer, and/or a spring mulch, helps keep it in good condition.

GROWING METHOD

Propagation Grow from semi-ripe tip cuttings taken in the summer. Alternatively use hardwood cuttings taken in the winter.

Spacing Plants can be spaced at 40–50cm (16–20in) intervals to achieve a good, thick hedge.

Feeding Can be grown without supplementary fertilizer. If the soil is very poor, apply all-purpose plant food in spring.

Problems There are no known problems.

FLOWERING

Season Flowers appear in midsummer. Many people find the scent unpleasant and overpowering.

PRUNING

General As the growth of this plant is particularly rapid, privet needs to be trimmed frequently. Cut out any growths that you can see are reverting to plain green. As flowers appear, shear or tip prune to avoid fruit setting.

LONICERA NITIDA
Honeysuckle

TINY, CLOSE-GROWING LEAVES make this an ideal choice for hedging where a tight formal shape is wanted.

A GAP in this honeysuckle hedge allows access to an enclosed garden and frames a young crab-apple tree.

FEATURES

Formal

This small-leaved, dense evergreen plant is sometimes known as box-leaf honeysuckle. It is quick growing but also long lived. While plants can reach almost 2.4m (8ft) in height, they are most often seen hedged at about 50cm (20in) or even less. Honeysuckle is an ideal shrub for formal hedges around garden beds or, when it is allowed to grow taller, for dividing sections of a garden or accenting a path or drive. It can also be clipped to various shapes for topiary. Honeysuckle bears strongly perfumed cream flowers during the late spring and early summer, although few blooms appear if the plants are kept close clipped.

LONICERA AT A GLANCE

Lonicera nitida is a highly valued, quick growing, scented evergreen shrub with blue berries. Hardy to −18°C (0°F).

JAN	foliage 🌱	COMPANION PLANTS
FEB	foliage 🌱	*Campsis radicans*
MAR	foliage 🌱	Clematis
APRIL	foliage 🌱	Climbing rose
MAY	flowering ❀	*Cobaea scandens*
JUNE	flowering ❀	Ipomoea
JULY	foliage 🌱	Jasmine
AUG	foliage 🌱	*Lonicera similis* var. *delavayi*
SEPT	foliage 🌱	Tropaeolum
OCT	foliage 🌱	
NOV	foliage 🌱	
DEC	foliage 🌱	

CONDITIONS

Aspect   Prefers an open, sunny position but will also tolerate some partial shade.

Site   The soil should be well drained but need not be rich, although soil that is high in organic content will give more vigorous growth and a better display of white flowers.

GROWING METHOD

Propagation   Can be grown from firm tip cuttings taken in early or midsummer.

Spacing   For a quick effect, honeysuckle can be planted at 25cm (10in) spacings, but 45cm (18in) might be more sensible.

Feeding   Apply complete plant food in early spring.

Problems   There are no known problems, but keep an eye out for aphid attacks.

FLOWERING

Season   Small, perfumed, creamy flowers appear in late spring and early summer. However, if the plants are clipped regularly through the growing season flowers may not develop.

PRUNING

General   To maintain low, dense growth honeysuckle needs regular clipping throughout the growing season; up to three cuttings in a season is quite typical.

OLEARIA X HAASTII
Daisy bush

MIDSUMMER IS that much brighter when you have an Olearia x haastii's *blinding white blooms glinting under the blue sky.*

THE FLOWERS of O. x haastii *develop through the season, before giving way to the fluffy, brown seedheads, providing interesting texture.*

FEATURES

Informal

If you need a highly unusual idea for a flowering hedge, this is it. A New Zealand bushy shrub with small, dark green leaves in the spring, and a white felt-like covering beneath. It is grown for its big show of white starry flowers in mid- and late summer, and the scent is a bit like that of hawthorn. The flowers are followed by brown fluffy seedheads. It grows at least 1.2m (4ft) high, and easily as wide, so just five plants would create an impressive summer windbreak hedge. It can be livened up with climbers like clematis and honeysuckle. A nearby purple *Buddleja davidii*, flowering at the same time, gives a strong contrast of colours. Despite its southern origins, this olearia is perfectly hardy.

OLEARIA AT A GLANCE

Olearia x *haastii* is a bushy shrub with a big summer show of daisy-like white flowers. Thrives in coastal areas. Hardy to −15°C (5°F).

JAN	foliage ✿	COMPANION PLANTS	
FEB	foliage ✿	Clematis	
MAR	foliage ✿	*Cobaea scandens*	
APRIL	foliage ✿	Ipomoea	
MAY	foliage ✿	Lapageria	
JUNE	foliage ✿	Passion flower	
JULY	flowering ❀	Rose	
AUG	flowering ❀	Tropaeolum	
SEPT	foliage ✿		
OCT	foliage ✿		
NOV	foliage ✿		
DEC	foliage ✿		

CONDITIONS

Aspect   Full sun gives the best display of flowers. Do not hide theses shrubs away in the shade.

Site   The more sun the better.

GROWING METHOD

Propagation   The best results are from summer cuttings, which are semi-ripe, in pots of cuttings compost. They should take quite quickly. Give frost-protection the first winter, for planting out the following spring.

Spacing   Set plants from 60–90cm (2–3ft) apart.

Feeding   A spring application of a slow-release fertilizer should suffice. The ground should have been well prepared before planting, with generous quantities of well-rotted organic matter. Make sure there is good drainage.

Problems   Olearia is virtually trouble-free. An easy grow, low-maintenance shrub.

FLOWERING

Season   *Olearia* x *haastii* flowers at the height of summer, and makes an incredible sight when, as an enormous hedge, it is in full flower. Contrasting coloured climbers can easily be grown through it.

PRUNING

General   Only needed to keep the plant in shape, or remove frost damage. If cutting to restrict size, prune up to one-third of last year's growth.

PHOTINIA
Photinia

FLUFFY, CREAMY-WHITE FLOWERS can be profuse on unpruned photinia. Few, if any, are seen on a formally trained hedge.

THE BRIGHT CRIMSON-PINK new growth on this photinia hedge makes a magnificent contribution to the garden.

FEATURES

Formal or
Informal

Evergreen and deciduous photinias, with their dense foliage, are among the most popular of hedging plants. The dark green, slightly leathery foliage is highlighted by bright pinky-red new growth. If the plant is trimmed regularly, this new growth is evident throughout the growing season. In spring and summer clusters of small white flowers appear. If unpruned, most bushes will grow to 3–5m (10–15ft) high but they can be hedged at around 2m (6ft). Photinias do, however, make very fine tall hedges and windbreaks. These plants are moderate growers and will be long lived if grown in suitable conditions.

PHOTINIA AT A GLANCE

Highly under-used shrubs giving marvellous fresh new growth, often vividly coloured, and early season white flowers. Hardy to –15°C (5°F).

		COMPANION PLANTS
JAN	foliage ❀	Anemone
FEB	foliage ❀	Bluebell
MAR	foliage ❀	Crocus
APRIL	flowering ❀	Daffodil
MAY	flowering ❀	Erythronium
JUNE	flowering ❀	Fritillaria
JULY	flowering ❀	Hyacinth
AUG	foliage ❀	Iris
SEPT	foliage ❀	Scilla
OCT	foliage ❀	Tulip
NOV	foliage ❀	
DEC	foliage ❀	

CONDITIONS

Aspect	Needs to be grown in full sun. Will also tolerate some degree of partial shade.
Site	Soil must be well drained and ideally should contain plenty of organic matter.

GROWING METHOD

Propagation	Can be grown from semi-ripe cuttings taken during the summer.
Spacing	Plant at about 1m (3ft) spacings.
Feeding	Apply complete plant food during the spring and summer growing season.
Problems	Photinias have no specific pest problems but will quickly succumb to root rot in heavy, poorly drained soil. It is therfore essential that you do not grow them in cold wet clay.

FLOWERING

Season	Clusters of white flowers appear during spring. One of the earliest is *Photinia* x *fraseri*, *P. glabra* flowers in early summer, and *P. nussia* in mid-summer.
Cutting	Flowers are not suitable for cutting.

PRUNING

General	Carry out the main pruning in late winter but lighter pruning can be done at other times of the year. Light summer pruning promotes plenty of attractive young foliage.

POTENTILLA FRUTICOSA
Cinquefoil

CATCHING THE LATE afternoon sun, these flowers of Potentilla
fruticosa *make bright yellow highlights among the dark green foliage.*

THERE ARE MANY colours of P. fruticosa *varieties to choose from.
This one,* P. f. *'Tangerine' has rich yellow/orange flowers.*

FEATURES

Informal

This is a small, easy-care, informal flowering
shrub. It grows about 1m (3ft) high and has
masses of yellow flowers from late spring right
through to mid-autumn. It can be grown in
one long yellow hedge, but looks best in a
sequence of different potentillas. Look for
those flowering in contrasting red, pink, white
and orange, but make sure that they all grow
to, or can be pruned to, the same height. All
you need do is give them the gentlest late
winter prune all over to stimulate plenty of
new growth. The flowers appear on the current
season's growth. When buying a potentilla
look at the label carefully since some only
grow 10cm (4in) high.

POTENTILLA AT A GLANCE

Potentilla fruticosa makes the perfect small, informal, flowery hedge. It
has many excellent forms. Hardy to −15°C (5°F).

JAN	/	RECOMMENDED VARIETIES
FEB	/	*Potentilla fruticosa* 'Daydawn'
MAR	/	P. f. 'Friedrichsenii'
APR	/	P. f. 'Goldfinger'
MAY	flowering ❀	P. f. 'Katherine Dykes'
JUN	flowering ❀	P. f. 'Maanelys'
JULY	flowering ❀	
AUG	flowering ❀	COMPANION PLANTS
SEP	flowering ❀	Box
OCT	flowering ❀	Fuchsia
NOV	/	Lavender
DEC	/	

CONDITIONS

Aspect   The plants generally prefer full sun, but will
tolerate partial shade.

Site   Over-rich soil is not necessary. Potentillas
prefer the ground to be slightly on the poor
side, with excellent drainage. Clay soil must be
well broken up with plenty of added
horticultural sand and grit.

GROWING METHOD

Propagation   The quickest methods are either by division in
the spring or autumn, or taking cuttings in the
first part of summer. They strike very quickly.

Spacing   Plant at 60cm (2ft) intervals, allowing each
plant to grow about 1.2m (4ft) wide.

Feeding   They benefit from a feed in the spring of a
slow-release fertilizer.

Problems   There are no known problems.

FLOWERING

Season   An exceptional flowering period, with the
yellow flowers in bloom from the spring,
through summer, into the autumn. The
flowers, which resemble small wild roses, have
five petals – hence the name cinquefoil.

PRUNING

General   In the autumn, after flowering, prune for shape
and to take out any old, dead or twiggy wood.
Give a light late winter prune if necessary.

PRUNUS LAUROCERASUS
Cherry laurel

CHERRY LAUREL makes a rather massive hedge, providing good shelter for an exposed garden. The dry-stone wall adds a rustic touch.

KEPT AT FENCE HEIGHT, this cherry laurel hedge will allow tantalising glimpses into the lovely garden behind.

FEATURES

Formal

If left unpruned, cherry laurel grows into a tree-like shape, but pruned it makes an imposing hedge for a larger garden, most often to about 3m (10ft), thus providing privacy and a windbreak. The evergreen foliage is dark green and glossy; perfumed white flowers are followed by red, cherry-like fruits. This is a very long-lived plant. There are a number of excellent cultivars available.

CONDITIONS

Aspect   Grows in sun or partial shade.
Site   This plant prefers to root into well-drained soil that is heavily enriched with decayed organic matter. Therefore, avoid the two extremes of nutritionless, free-draining chalk soil and a heavy, wet, boggy ground.

GROWING METHOD

Propagation   Grow from semi-ripe tip cuttings that are taken in midsummer. It can also be grown from seed if the ripe berries are picked, cleaned of the pulp and then stored in damp sand or damp sphagnum moss in the refrigerator for about three months before they are sown.
Spacing   It should be planted at about 1m (3ft) spacings. Do not be tempted to plant any closer together because crowding them is counter-productive – give them space to grow.
Feeding   Apply plant food after spring flowering.
Problems   No specific problems are known.

FLOWERING

Season   The small, white, scented flowers appear in spring. However, flowers will not appear if the plant is pruned in late winter.
Berries   The flowers are followed by red berries that ripen to black. Birds love them. A good alternative to holly, box and yew.

PRUNING

General   If you want flowers, do your main pruning immediately after flowering has finished; otherwise it can be done in late winter. Other trimming can be done throughout the growing season if necessary.

PRUNUS AT A GLANCE

Prunus laurocerasus can make a 6m (20ft) high tree, but pruned is a fine, sturdy, thick hedge. Hardy to –18°C (0°F).

		COMPANION PLANTS
JAN	foliage	Anemone
FEB	foliage	Bluebell
MAR	foliage	Crocus
APR	flowering	Daffodil
MAY	flowering	Erythronium
JUN	foliage	Fritillaria
JULY	foliage	Hyacinth
AUG	foliage	Iris
SEP	foliage	Scilla
OCT	foliage	Tulip
NOV	foliage	
DEC	foliage	

PYRACANTHA
Firethorn

THE ABUNDANT CLUSTERS of bright fruits on this firethorn provide a wonderful bounty during the autumn months.

OCCASIONAL PRUNING is enough to keep this firethorn hedge dense and attractive, easily fulfilling its role as boundary and screen.

FEATURES

Formal or Informal

These evergreen shrubs with thorny stems are often planted as hedges in rural areas, but they are just as much at home in suburban districts. Unpruned, they will be 2–3m (6½–10ft) high but are often pruned to less than that. Firethorns are fairly fast growing but are also long lived. The leaves are glossy and clusters of small, white flowers appear in spring or early summer. These are soon followed by bright red or orange berries (the 'fire' of the firethorn) which are very decorative and most attractive to birds. Branches of the bright red or orange berries can be cut for indoor decoration once they are fully coloured. Be careful where you plant it though because the sharp pointed spines are dangerous.

PYRACANTHA AT A GLANCE

High quality berrying plants that make an eye-catching hedge. Beware of the spines though. Hardy to –15°C (5°F).

JAN	foliage ❄	RECOMMENDED VARIETIES
FEB	foliage ❄	*Pyracantha coccinea* 'Red
MAR	foliage ❄	Column'
APR	flowering ✳	P. 'Golden Charmer'
MAY	flowering ✳	P. 'Mohave'
JUN	flowering ✳	P. 'Orange Glow'
JULY	flowering ✳	*P. rogersiana*
AUG	foliage ❄	*P. rogersiana* 'Flava'
SEP	foliage ❄	P. 'Soleil d'Or'
OCT	foliage ❄	P. 'Watereri'
NOV	foliage ❄	
DEC	foliage ❄	

CONDITIONS

Aspect Needs full sun and tolerates exposure to wind. Will tolerate some partial shade.

Site Grows on a wide range of soils, including poor soils, but best growth will be in those enriched with organic matter. For a good show of bright coloured berries, rich soil is best.

GROWING METHOD

Propagation Grow from seed removed from ripe berries and planted fresh. Plants can also be grown from semi-ripe cuttings taken in summer.

Spacing Plant at intervals of 70cm–1m (28in–3ft).

Feeding Feeding is not essential, but on poor soils give complete plant food in early spring.

Problems They suffer from a range of pests and diseases like caterpillars, scale, canker, and fireblight.

FLOWERING

Season The white flowers appear in the spring (*Pyracantha rogersiana*), early summer (*P.* 'Orange Charmer'), and mid-summer (*P. angustifolia*). Although they provide a good show, they are outdone by the brilliant berries.

Berries The flowers are followed by clusters of berries that will ripen to a blazing red, orange or yellow, depending on the species.

PRUNING

General Best pruned in spring. Start training and pruning in the first couple of years of growth.

RHODODENDRON
'Loder's White'

THE FLOWERS of the rhododendron are among the most sumptuous to be found. And this Rhododendron 'Loder's White' is no exception to the rule. The frilly petals are set off by delicate stamen to create a delightful texture. The blooms time their appearance to perfection, enjoying the midsummer sun.

FEATURES

Informal

Rhododendrons come in all shapes and sizes, from 1m (3ft) high to tree-like giants growing 6m (20ft) or so. They are traditionally grown as individual eyecatchers, with a big show of flowers anytime from late autumn to late summer, though the bulk perform in the spring and early summer. They can also make thick hedges or windbreaks, in the case of *Rhododendron* 'Loder's White' about 2.4m (8ft) high and wide. You need a big garden, and one with acid soil. The plants also need dappled shade, and protection from cold winds. With adequate space, grow different coloured rhododendrons to make a patchwork effect. It is worth visiting a specialist collection to see the full range now available.

RHODODENDRON AT A GLANCE

Rhododendron 'Loder's White' is a fine plant, giving an excellent display packed with scented white flowers. Hardy to –15°C (5°F).

JAN	foliage 🌿	RECOMMENDED VARIETIES
FEB	foliage 🌿	*Rhododendron* 'Anna Rose
MAR	foliage 🌿	Whitney'
APR	foliage 🌿	*R.* 'Blue Peter'
MAY	foliage 🌿	*R.* 'Cynthia'
JUN	flowering ✿	*R.* 'Gomer Waterer'
JULY	flowering ✿	*R.* 'Hydon Dawn'
AUG	foliage 🌿	*R.* 'Kilimanjaro'
SEP	foliage 🌿	*R.* 'Loderi King George'
OCT	foliage 🌿	*R.* 'Mrs Furnival'
NOV	foliage 🌿	*R.* 'Razorbill'
DEC	foliage 🌿	

CONDITIONS

Aspect Sun with dappled shade is ideal, approaching a light woodland setting. Avoid both full sun and constant shade.

Site Acid soil is absolutely essential. Individual plants can be grown in tubs with ericaceous compost. Trying to turn an alkaline garden area acid by adding replacement acid soil might work for one season, but thereafter the surrounding alkaline soil will gradually seep back in, and the rhododendrons will falter.

GROWING METHOD

Propagation Take semi-ripe cuttings from midsummer.

Spacing *R.* 'Loder's White' should be spaced about 1.2m (4ft) apart. Do not try and plant them any closer together. Each shrub needs to be able to show off all its flowers.

Feeding Give an annual mulch using leaf mould.

FLOWERING

Season It flowers right in the middle of summer, at the height of the season. After flowering, attempt to deadhead as much as possible to preserve energy for next year's display. Adding other rhododendrons that flower in early and late summer will extend the show.

PRUNING

General Leave to realize its full potential. It will automatically thicken up and get quite bushy.

ROSA RUGOSA
Rose

THE DELICATE PURPLE hues of this plant's flowers belie the tough nature of Rosa rugosa, *able to survive in exposed positions.*

WITH THEIR ORANGE centres, R. rugosa *flowers are a pleasant feature of the garden from early summer right through to the autumn.*

FEATURES

Informal

Flowering hedges are making a comeback, and one of the best involves *Rosa rugosa*. It grows about 2.1m (7ft) high and wide, and makes a good, tough barrier. Extremely hardy, bushy, and tolerant of coastal winds and sandy soils (it dislikes clay instead), this rose scores high marks. It also has a long purple-rose flowering season from early summer, large cherry-red hips, and even autumn colour. Two excellent forms of this useful species are 'Alba', with single white flowers against dark green leaves, and the crimson-wine 'Rubra'. The cross between *R. rugosa* and *R. wichurana* led to 'Max Graf', which is quite different and makes a good weed-obscuring groundcover, about 60cm (2ft) high. It does not make a hedge. Other crosses involving *R. rugosa* have produced many excellent shrub roses, especially the white 'Blanc Double de Coubert', which grows 1.8m (6ft) high.

ROSA AT A GLANCE

Rosa rugosa is an excellent multi-purpose shrub, giving great flowers and sweet scent right through the summer. Hardy to −18°C (0°F).

JAN	/	COMPANION PLANTS
FEB	/	Clematis
MAR	/	Crocus
APRIL	foliage 🌿	Cyclamen
MAY	foliage 🌿	Erythronium
JUNE	flowering ✽	Ipomoea
JULY	flowering ✽	Primrose
AUG	flowering ✽	Winter jasmine
SEPT	flowering ✽	
OCT	flowering ✽	
NOV	/	
DEC	/	

CONDITIONS

Aspect Provide full sun, or at the very least dappled shade. The sunnier the garden, the better.

Site Famed for growing in sandy soils, average garden conditions are fine. So too are beds with deep rich soil and plenty of humus, though sound drainage is always required. The plant does not like heavy clay soils, and these will need to be broken up and lightened so that water drains away more freely.

GROWING METHOD

Propagation In the autumn take 20cm- (8in-) long hardwood cuttings, and set in trenches with the top quarter showing above soil level. They make roots slowly and will be ready to plant out the following autumn.

Spacing Set *R. rugosa* about 1.2m (4ft) apart.

Feeding Feeding twice a summer with a proprietary rose feed will be fine. Also, mulch with well-rotted organic matter.

Problems No serious problems that should alarm potential growers.

FLOWERING

Season An excellent extended season, with long, pointed buds. Though the flowers can be short-lived in hot weather, there is no let-up in the development of more buds.

PRUNING

General Not necessary beyond giving a light trim in February to promote plenty of fresh new shoots. At the same time remove old, unproductive stems or those that have died.

ROSMARINUS
Rosemary

THE INTENSE LIGHT blue of this Rosmarinus officinalis *'Miss Jessopp's Upright' seems to explode from a plain, red brick wall.*

FRESH NEW SHOOTS of rosemary respond to a light pruning. A few plants should keep a whole household supplied with the delicious herb.

FEATURES

Informal

Rosemary makes an excellent edging-cum-hedging plant. The big problem is that it is quite slow growing, so do not count on a sudden, big thick hedge packed with scented leaves. It will gradually give a 1.2m (4ft) high tangle of stems, and marvellous pale blue flowers from early spring. Since there are about 20 kinds of *Rosmarinus officinalis* you could create a long stretch with as many tall kinds as you can collect. 'Tuscan Blue' has strong, dark blue flowers, 'Roseus' pink flowers, *R. o.* var. *albiflorus* is white, and 'Sissinghurst Blue' is extremely free-flowering. Note that some like 'Benenden Blue' grow just 90cm (3ft) high, and others ('Majorca Pink') are even shorter at 45cm (18in).

ROSMARINUS AT A GLANCE

Rosmarinus officinalis 'Miss Jessopp's Upright' is a 'must' for the edible garden. Hardy to −10°C (14°F).

JAN	foliage	RECOMMENDED VARIETIES
FEB	foliage	*Rosmarinus officinalis*
MAR	foliage	*R. o.* var. *albiflorus*
APRIL	flowering	*R. o.* 'Aureus'
MAY	flowering	*R. o.* 'Fota Blue'
JUNE	flowering	*R. o.* 'McConnell's Blue'
JULY	foliage	*R. o.* 'Miss Jessopp's
AUG	foliage	Upright'
SEPT	foliage	*R. o.* 'Prostratus Group'
OCT	foliage	*R. o.* 'Severn Sea'
NOV	foliage	*R. o.* 'Sissinghurst Blue'
DEC	foliage	*R. o.* 'Tuscan Blue'

Aspect Full sun is required. These Mediterranean plants need as much light as they can get.

Site Anything from quite poor, stony ground to average fertility. The most important point is that they receive good drainage. They will not enjoy heavy, cold, wet clay.

GROWING METHOD

Propagation Take semi-ripe cuttings through the summer season. It is an inexpensive, if slow way of creating new plants. If you can afford it, buy large-sized specimens giving an instant effect.

Spacing 'Miss Jessopp's Upright' is one of the tallest rosemarys at 1.5m (5ft). Space individual plants at half that distance.

Feeding Not necessary except on the poorest of soils.

Problems Rosemary is a remarkably easy-care plant, and suffers from very few setbacks.

FLOWERING

Season The show of pale blue flowers from early spring, near adjacent daffodils, gives the garden an excellent boost.

PRUNING

General The only form of pruning required is to snip back lanky stems in the spring. Regular summer snippings for the kitchen will see to the rest. Old overgrown plants can be cut back by half, and will reshoot. If you need rosemary for cooking the more plants you grow the better, or young ones quickly get massacred.

TAXUS BACCATA
Yew

MATURE YEW PLANTS *have sombre, dark green foliage but new spring growth, such as that shown here, is much brighter.*

YEW IS *the ideal hedging plant for cool climates. Formal shapes can be achieved and maintained over a long time.*

FEATURES

Formal

The English yew is extremely long lived and fairly slow growing, but it makes a dense hedge that can be closely clipped. It is also widely used in topiary, and there are specimens that have been clipped for several hundred years. In Britain and Europe yew hedges have been traditionally used to shelter herbaceous borders or as a background for statuary and garden ornaments. Foliage is dark and evergreen, and it produces a red fleshy fruit that is quite poisonous. Unpruned trees may grow to 15m (50ft) or more but yew is generally hedged at about 2.4m (8ft). There are a number of cultivars of yew, providing many variations in form and foliage colour.

TAXUS AT A GLANCE

Taxus baccata provides a traditional, strong, formal hedge that can easily be topiarized to give geometric shapes. Hardy to –18°C (0°F).

JAN	foliage	RECOMMENDED VARIETIES
FEB	foliage 🍃	*Taxus baccata*
MAR	foliage 🍃	*T. b.* 'Adpressa'
APRIL	flowering ❋	*T. b.* 'Fastigiata'
MAY	flowering ❋	*T. b.* 'Fastigiata Aurea'
JUNE	foliage 🍃	*T. b.* 'Fastigiata
JULY	foliage 🍃	Aureomarginata'
AUG	foliage 🍃	*T.* x *media*
SEPT	foliage 🍃	*T.* x *media* 'Brownii'
OCT	foliage 🍃	
NOV	foliage 🍃	
DEC	foliage 🍃	

CONDITIONS

Aspect Prefers an open, sunny position. This plant is tolerant of windy sites.

Site Soil should be well drained and enriched with organic matter. Mulch around plants with decayed manure or compost. It is tempting to plant yew and then completely forget about it, but good care yields fine, dense growth.

GROWING METHOD

Propagation Take firm cuttings with a heel of older wood in autumn. These may not be well rooted until the following summer. Use a hormone rooting gel or powder to increase the strike rate.

Spacing Yew can be planted at 50cm–1m (20in–3ft) spacings, depending on the density required.

Feeding Apply complete plant food or slow-release fertilizer in spring.

Problems There are no specific problems. Yew is an easy-care, reliable shrub or small tree.

FLOWERING

Products Yew is a conifer, not a flowering plant. It produces very small cones in season as well as bright red, poisonous fruits.

PRUNING

General To create your hedge, prune little and often. However, yew can be cut back severely and still regenerate well.

VIBURNUM TINUS
Laurustinus

LAURUSTINUS is not often seen grown as a standard but, in fact, it responds well to this form of training.

THIS FORMAL HEDGE of laurustinus is healthy and flourishing. It needs little pruning apart from trimming to shape.

FEATURES

Formal or Informal

This is a dense, evergreen shrub that needs little training to make a good hedge. It is reasonably fast growing and long lived in good conditions. Laurustinus bears masses of small white flowers with a pink base during late winter and spring. The flowers are followed by berries, which ripen to blue-black. This shrub can grow to 3m (10ft) high but can be kept at about 2m (6ft). It is generally easy to care for.

CONDITIONS

Aspect   *Viburnum tinus* prefers sites with full sun.

VIBURNUM AT A GLANCE

Viburnum tinus is a fine evergreen shrub, with a mass of white, late winter flowers. Makes excellent topiary. Hardy to –18°C (0°F).

JAN	foliage ❀	RECOMMENDED VARIETIES
FEB	flowering ❀	*V.* x *bodnantense* 'Dawn'
MAR	flowering ❀	*Viburnum* x *burkwoodii*
APRIL	flowering ❀	*V.* x *burkwoodii* 'Anne
MAY	foliage ❀	Russell'
JUNE	foliage ❀	*V.* x *burkwoodii* 'Fullbrook'
JULY	foliage ❀	*V. davidii*
AUG	foliage ❀	*V. japonicum*
SEPT	foliage ❀	*V. odoratissimum*
OCT	foliage ❀	*V. plicatum* 'Grandiflorum'
NOV	foliage ❀	
DEC	foliage ❀	

Site   Needs well-drained soil that has been enriched with organic matter.

GROWING METHOD

Propagation   Grow from semi-ripe cuttings taken in the summer. Plants can also be grown from cleaned seed collected in the autumn and stored in damp sphagnum moss in the refrigerator until spring.

Spacing   Planting should be at about 1m (3ft) intervals, but can be closer if cover is needed quickly.

Feeding   Apply all-purpose plant food in spring.

Problems   The main problems to look out for are viburnum beetles, aphids, whiteflies and honey fungus. The first damage leaves mainly from late spring to early summer. Treat with a proprietary spray. The second and third are easily tackled, again with chemical measures. The fourth is a big problem. It involves discarding the entire plant, with stump. Fortify the soil with organic matter, and replant with box, bamboo or chaenomeles.

FLOWERING

Season   Small flowers appear in late winter and spring.

Berries   The flowers are followed by berries that ripen in autumn to a blue-black colour.

PRUNING

General   Best done after spring flowering.

GROWING LAWNS

A lawn can mean different things to different people. It may be the showpiece of your garden, a foil for displays of flowering shrubs and annuals, a piece of grass on which to sit, or even the chance to create something very special, like a medieval turf maze, with concentric rings of raised grass.

Whatever your lawn means to you, you will need to spend time maintaining it. This is the case even if, like most gardeners, you are content if your lawn grows reasonably well and is not too overrun with weeds. If you want to go further and achieve the perfection of a velvety smooth, immaculate lawn, you will need to put in a great deal of time and effort. Lawns are a long-term investment in terms of time and money.

LEFT: Very closely mown turf is used to top the walls of this highly decorative maze. The neat, dense-growing bent grasses are used for their high tolerance of intensive culture and mowing.

A BROAD SWEEP OF LAWN is here edged and defined with a range of perennial plants and punctuated by trees. The open space thus created gives a welcoming appearance to the property, allowing an uninterrupted view of the house from the entrance.

PLANNING A LAWN

Don't rush into establishing your lawn: taking time to plan it carefully will pay off in the long run. Ensure the soil is well prepared and consider the climate, the amount of direct sun the area receives and the primary use the lawn will have. There are grasses that withstand heavy wear and grasses that cope with shade, but it is virtually impossible to find a grass that does both and no turf will withstand constant rough usage from large dogs or daily football games without looking the worse for wear.

Plan your lawn area so that it will be easy to mow and maintain. Avoid sharp corners as it is easier to mow around curved edges, and don't have lots of small garden beds—they not only make mowing difficult but spoil the effect of a sweeping lawn. Concrete mower strips reduce the amount of time and effort needed to trim edges but should not be put in until after the turf has been established. If they are installed before the turf and the soil subsides they will be more of a hindrance than a help.

Lawn shape and style
The kind of lawn you need will largely be determined by the style of your garden. A smart, formal garden with topiary and statuary needs an equally formal area of lawn setting off these grand effects.

The lawn should lead up to and away from such eyecatchers. If the overall effect is not to be ruined, the grass needs regular mowing, but not so short that the roots fail to grow down, resulting in dusty brown patches in long, hot dry spells. The root system will not go down deep enough to find water and you will end up having to water it for hours on a regular basis. The lawn edges also need to be well maintained. They should be sharp and smart, and clearly defined, generally in long straight lines.

Cottage gardens, on the other hand, are far more informal and unpredictable. They do not demand a perfect lawn that needs regular preening. Let daisies and buttercups grow (both are highly underrated and really give a lawn beautiful colouring), allowing the grass to flow between the beds. Such lawns need not try and hog the limelight, but can act as informal areas between great sweeps of flowers. They can meander round the garden, and form separate areas, the only key consideration being to check that where the lawn becomes a sudden narrow path there is still enough room for your mower. Also, check that the design is not so curvy that mowing becomes extremely tricky and you end up having to clip certain areas of grass with sheers.

It helps if all lawns, whether formal or cottage, are either hemmed in by paths or specially made long thin strips of metal to stop the grass invading the beds. Otherwise they will need regular attention with an edging 'slicer'. In big gardens this can take several hours unless you use a powered edger. Cottage gardens might be low maintenance, but they too need plenty of attention if the casual look is not to turn into the uncontrollably impossible and ramshackle.

PATHS AND FRAMING

One of the most poorly thought out aspects of any garden is the path. Too often it is just seen as a means of getting from A to B, the outdoor equivalent of a corridor. Yet details like paths really stand out in the garden, especially in winter when most of the plant areas are not performing and the flowers have all gone. Then the structural details such as paths, trellises and steps stand out like the bones on an x-ray. And there is no reason at all why a path should not be as smart, as engaging and as well constructed as any part of the garden.

Paths can be entirely of grass, and if they are infrequently used and do not become worn out, they can easily become star features of a garden. A tongue of green between island beds, especially first thing in the morning when covered with dew, or after they have been mowed when they have a fresh green colour, is a real thrill. And such paths can easily be styled.

Japanese type gardens often use grass paths with interlocking sections decorated with different patterns of stone. In effect that means there might be 6m (20ft) of path with large stones set to the left-hand side only in patterned groupings that keep repeating themselves. The next section of grass path has larger or smaller stones or rocks, but this time to the other side, in slightly different arrangements. Such patterning guarantees that the garden works at every level.

With more formal gardens the grass can give way to arrangements of frost-proof brick, using patterns like herringbone. You can also use different coloured bricks to heighten the effect. And paths around a lawn help to frame and lift it. The edges do not fall away and disappear into adjacent beds, but they are well defined and stand out with clarity, giving the whole area an air of neatness.

THIS PATH HAS a gentle curve that helps it to blend in with the garden, and also serves to highlight the lawn, archway and borders. The shape will also make it more pleasing when the garden dies down.

GRASS IS A VERSATILE medium. Here it has been used to create a sort of half-lawn, half-paved area. Squares of tough glass are framed by strips of grass, the rich green of the plant setting off the light turquoise of the glass. This arrangement gives the whole garden a thoroughly modern look.

Choosing a grass

Grasses for lawns fall into two main categories. First, there are those for use in the high quality showpiece lawn. These are intended to be areas that visitors are definitely not allowed to walk on. It has much the same function and eyecatching appeal as a flowerbed. Its principal aim is to make the onlooker gasp. And there is nothing wrong with a superbly well-manicured, neatly clipped bowling green, even when it is in your garden. These lawns are maintenance heavy, but are of course infinitely rewarding. They should be lush green and provide an effective contrast to formal beds and borders. The second type of lawn is the utility area, which can be anything from an attractive sheet of green to a mock cricket pitch. These are areas that are intended to be used and need to be able to stand up to some pretty tough treatment. Nevertheless, these lawns will also benefit from some love and attention. The key point is to make sure you choose the appropriate grass. The latter case demands hard-wearing grasses that will withstand everything thrown at them, while the former demands high quality good-looking cover. Grass seed is generally sold as one or the other, though specialist suppliers can easily make up a mix tailor-made according to your special needs.

PREPARING THE SOIL

Friable sandy loam is the best soil on which to establish turf but few of us are blessed with this ideal situation. It may be necessary to create these conditions, or as close to them as possible, before planting or laying a lawn. Soil needs to be loose and workable to a depth of 15–25cm (6–10in). If you have a clay subsoil you may need to bring in extra soil and cover the whole area to be turfed to a depth of at least 10cm (4in). Try to get a guarantee from the soil supplier that the soil is weed-free, and check that the soil is not full of silty clay that will set like cement when it dries after watering.

You cannot simply place the imported soil on top of the clay as this would cause drainage problems and prevent penetration of grass roots into the clay layer. Added soil must be well mixed with the existing soil so that no barrier will form.

Heavy clay soils are best treated with an application of gypsum, about 300g per sq/m (10oz per 10sq/ft), or if the soil is known to be very acid, garden or agricultural lime can be applied at 100g per sq/m (3oz per 10sq/ft). Clay soils should never be cultivated when they are very wet or very dry—they need to be just moist. The incorporation

A SIMPLE BRICK BORDER works wonders for this lawn. The bricks not only serve to keep the lawn in place and stop it spilling into the surrounding beds, but also act as a framing device, creating an aesthetic space between the grass and the busy plantings.

of large quantities of organic matter into the soil well ahead of laying or sowing the turf will also help to improve aeration and soil drainage.

Sandy soils should be prepared by adding copious amounts of well-decayed manure or compost to aid water and nutrient retention, and the area to be turfed should be free of stones, roots and any other debris.

Tackling Weeds

There is nothing worse for a gardener than going to the toil and trouble of creating a lush new lawn, only to find that the whole area is riddled with tough weeds. Be sure to remove all weeds before the lawn goes down, especially the perennial kind, otherwise they will spread and increase. When creating a new lawn it is worth spending every extra hour you can to eradicate possible future problems. Prepare the site of the lawn well in advance of seeding or laying turf so that you give the weeds plenty of time to appear. And as they keep appearing you can keep digging them out. But make sure that you do not leave behind even the tiniest piece of root because it can re-grow, and the problem will just re-emerge later. And whatever happens, do not allow weeds to flower and set seed, or you will have a massive problem that takes much longer to eradicate.

Emerging weeds on new lawns, provided there are not that many, are generally easily tackled. After a few years the lawn should be virtually weed free, though especially in the countryside there is always the chance that unwanted seeds from weeds in neighbouring fields will blow in and establish themselves. Vigilance is the only solution to this problem or perhaps a sensibly lax attitude arguing it really does not matter that much if a lawn does have weeds. It is only a problem when you end up with big rosettes of thistles which make it impossible to lie down and sleep, and plantains start to take over, blocking out the grass. When a lawn stops being what you want, then it is time to worry.

EVEN SMALL AREAS benefit from the addition of lawn. Here a circular green has been created with the use of a raised area bordered with attractive brickwork. It adds a sense of space to this small garden.

BROWNTOP BENT and highland bent grasses produce a very fine finish when grown in cool climate gardens.

STEPPING STONES are here set into a lush, thick cushion of bent grasses to prevent wear on the turf.

A MIXTURE OF cool season grasses is used to create this lawn. It looks so healthy, even though growing in a high-traffic area.

SITE LEVELLING

Though it sounds incredibly demanding, site levelling is really worthwhile because once the lawn is laid, it can be a huge job to modify or change it. Work carried out before the lawn goes down can save much toil later on.

If the site of the new lawn has too many bumps and dips, it means mowing might become extremely awkward. If the mower can't reach the grass in a slight hollow, the grass there will always be slightly longer than the rest of the lawn. It also means that mowing becomes a nightmare because the machine keeps tilting over at angles, even scalping the grass as it suddenly comes into close contact with it. And children's games are never quite what they should be when half the 'pitch' is dead flat, the other all bumps and rises, and then a sudden slope running away.

You can level the site professionally by taking measurements, but many gardeners find that it can be done nearly as well by eye. It simply requires a strong back and a spade to work right over the area. While you are filling in or levelling holes and bumps, keep standing back and checking the area is flat. Then rake over the soil, and firm it down by walking on it with a large pair of heavy old boots. Rake a second time with a finer rake, and then again flatten the soil.

The next key stage is to make sure that you have applied a fertilizer of blood and bone to the area according to label directions and lightly raked or watered it in. Water the area lightly for a few days before sowing the seed or laying the turf. This will firm the soil and provide a moist layer on which the grass can establish.

Drainage

Check the drainage of the area where the lawn is to go. Dig a hole, fill it with water and see how long it takes for the water to drain away. If water remains in the hole for more than 24 hours, you will have to consider laying subsoil drains or creating a slight slope on the area. A slope of 1 in 70 is sufficient to prevent the formation of wet spots, or you can install one of the do-it-yourself drainage systems that are are available from garden centres and hardware stores.

Problems tend to occur where there are spots of the lawn that stay wet for a long time after wet weather, because the grass may suffer from root rot and die out. And if there is any traffic over these wet areas the soil will rapidly become compacted, thus depriving the roots of air and leading to very poor growth.

CHOOSING THE RIGHT TURF

When selecting turf (note it is more expensive than seed because it gives an instant finish and involves more work on the part of the supplier) you are faced with the same decisions as when selecting the right seed mix. The choices are between showpiece top quality and everyday, multi-purpose lawns. Meadow turf is the cheapest kind, and you get what you pay for. In other words, it will be an interesting mixture of grasses, but will probably also be packed with weeds and coarse vigorous grasses, and the look is not that impressive. It is best to check it before buying. But if you need a tough lawn for children's games, etc, this is ideal. Sea-washed (or Sea Marsh) turf

BUSY PLANTINGS such as this one benefit from the addition of a lawn to act as a foil that helps to set off the various colours and shapes.

BOTH PRACTICAL and aesthetic, this lawn strip provides access to the long borders and highlights the variety of plants used.

THIS THIN STRIP of decorative lawn plays an essential part in the overall look of the garden. It helps to keep the heavily-planted garden from looking overcrowded. It also provides an area of brightness to contrast with some of the richer, darker colours used in the various plantings.

was once reckoned the Rolls Royce of turfs, with fescues and bents. It is rarely available now. Custom-made turf is specially grown to your own requirements.

Specialist suppliers often offer their own particular range of grasses, which basically divides into the elite or 'super lawn' category, and the hard-wearing. Ask to see a lawn they have recently laid to check it is what you want.

Turf or seed?
Lawns can be established by laying turf, for an instant finish, or sowing seed. The latter is less expensive but you need to keep off the sown area for several weeks.

LAYING TURF

Turf grass is living grass that is available in machine-cut rolls. It has been severed from most of its root system so it needs to be laid as soon as possible. Try to ensure that turf is delivered when you are ready for it. If there is any delay, keep the rolls in a shaded place and keep them damp.

To lay the rolls, place them on the prepared ground with their edges pushed firmly together. If the ground slopes, lay the rolls across the slope, not down it, to avoid erosion. It is a good idea to roll the newly laid turf to ensure good contact with the soil. Thoroughly water the

THIS BRIGHT GREEN expanse of lawn is growing in a cool, high rainfall area. In the foreground, young cherry trees provide shade.

A SMOOTH LAWN and standard 'Iceberg' roses flank the pool in this formal garden. Agapanthus and hydrangeas fill the foreground.

turf and keep it moist for the first 10–14 days. This may mean watering once a day in hot or windy weather. After this you can cut back to every second day.

Check whether or not the roots have taken by looking to see if the turf can be easily lifted from the soil. After about three weeks it should have become established and the regular watering can be reduced to a heavy soaking once a week, unless the weather is very hot. Mow lightly after about three weeks.

SOWING SEED

It can be difficult to sow grass seed evenly and so it is a good idea to mix the seed with some sand or dry sawdust. Divide the area to be sown into sections, and divide the seed into the same number of lots so that sowing can be fairly uniform. After sowing, lightly rake the seed into the surface soil and water gently, being careful not to allow pools to form that may wash the seed into patches. Seed sowing rates vary from grass to grass, so follow the directions on the packet.

You may need to water your newly sown lawn every day if the weather is windy or hot. The surface must be kept just moist at all times after seeding or results will be poor. Germination time varies with grass types and may be anywhere from five days to three weeks.

Grasses are usually sown in spring or autumn. The first light mowing should be carried out when the grass is 40–50mm (1½–2in) high.

MAINTENANCE

Mowing
As a general rule all lawns should be cut high rather than shaved. A handy hint is never to remove more than one-third of the leaf blade at any one cutting. If you mow the

lawn regularly in this way, you should soon have a healthy, dense, good-looking lawn. Here are some extra hints for a great lawn.

If grass has been allowed to grow very long it is better to reduce the height gradually rather than to cut it low with one mowing and risk scorching what is left.

Grass that is mown regularly will produce little in the way of clippings—there is no need to pick them up as they will break down very quickly in warm weather and return to the soil as humus.

As late autumn approaches, raise the mower height to help maintain the grass through the colder months.

Grass growing under trees should be cut very high, about 10cm (4in) high, if it is not to die out. Finally, it is not a good idea to mow when the grass is wet as this tends to tear the grass and clog the mower. Dry grass is easier to cut and you will get a better finish.

Topdressing
Topdressing has no intrinsic benefits for the lawn and is only necessary to fill in hollows and to maintain levels. It is best done in spring or early autumn. If there is a large hollow, apply only 2cm (¾in) of topdressing at a time and wait until the grass grows through it before applying more. Washed river sand or good quality sandy loam is best for topdressing. Never use builders' or bricklayers' sand as it sets like concrete.

Fertilizing
The average home lawn is probably fertilized only once or twice a year, in spring as new growth starts and again in late summer or early autumn. Very high quality lawns may need to be fertilized more often than this, perhaps every 4–6 weeks during the growing season. Use one of the many all-purpose lawn foods on the market, or pulverized poultry manure or blood and bone. In cases where fertilizers high in sulphate of ammonia have been

LAYING TURF

1. After checking the drainage, a prepared soil mix is brought to the site.

2. The soil is raked to make a level surface for turf. The soil should not be compacted.

3. Turf rolls are laid on the prepared soil. The edges are butted firmly together.

4. The turf is rolled to ensure good contact with the soil and eliminate air pockets.

5. The newly laid turf is fertilized. Some growers prefer to wait a few weeks.

6. The turf is thoroughly watered and the laying process is then complete.

A LAWN AND A DEEP HEDGE combine to give a pleasing strip effect, producing areas of calm and tranquility in the centre of this otherwise exuberant garden. Colours have been kept simple here, with a dominance of green and white, to increase their impact on the eye.

used frequently over a long period of time, the grass may benefit from a dressing of lime to counteract the acidity of the soil. This is best done during winter.

If the grass is turning a sickly yellow-green colour, it means that the lawn needs an extra nitrogen supplement. This is the nutrient that most commonly needs adding to the lawn. Apply it in spring and summer and the grass should soon turn rich green again. Do not apply it over winter as this will promote soft, loose growth that is prone to disease, and if adding it in the autumn make sure you do so in low quantities.

If the lawn seems rather feeble, it may be because it has always been so closely scalped and mown that the grass has not developed a deep root system. The answer is to mow higher and more infrequently, adding phosphates to boost root growth.

Potassium is rarely added alone, and is usually part of a general fertilizer mix that acts as an all-purpose tonic. Such cocktails commonly include iron, which helps darken the grass, giving it a healthier colour.

It is very easy to get worked up, fretting about the state of the lawn. The best general advice is to give it an all-purpose feed once or twice a year. If it looks healthy, has a good green colour and keeps you happy, why worry? And if you do need to fertilize, broadcast following the recommendations on the packet. If you have a large lawn

it may be worth buying a mechanical fertilizer spreader that delivers a set amount of fertilizer to an area while you walk along pushing it gently.

Watering

It is better to water heavily but infrequently. This encourages deep rooting of grasses that are better able to withstand drought. Grass that is watered heavily every week or 10 days is much stronger and healthier than grass that is given a daily sprinkle. That may be therapeutic for the gardener but it is bad news for the grass.

Bare patches

Bare spots in lawns may result from a number of things, including heavy wear, drying out or close mowing on uneven ground where there are high spots that get scalped. These spots cannot be repaired simply by putting fresh soil on top of the patch and hoping the grass will grow. You must dig over the area with a trowel or fork and either re-seed the area or plant runners. If you allow lawn edges to run, you will have a ready supply of runners for patching. Make a groove, slip the runner in at an angle and water in well. Or you can purchase a lawn repair kit from a garden centre. Kits contain seed pre-mixed in a sowing medium that is dyed bright green so that you can see where you have been sowing.

If the bare patches are in an area that receives heavy wear, such as the approach to a lawn or a clothes line, then it is probably best to replace that section of lawn with paving of some sort.

Depressions

Hollows can occur in both old and new lawns. They are especially likely in lawns laid by home-owners or by property developers doing a quick cosmetic job. They can be avoided by site levelling before laying the lawn. Topdressing can be used to fill in hollows in a lawn, but if the depression is deep, it will have to be filled gradually. Never apply more than 2cm (^{3}/$_4$in) of material at a time or you may kill the grass. You can add more topdressing every 10–14 days as grass grows through. Use washed river sand or good quality sandy loam. Spread the sand or loam and work it in with the back of a rake. Spring or autumn are the best times for this type of renovation.

Sparse lawns

Lawns can become thin and sparse for a number of reasons. The grass has been mown too low, usually over a long period. Constant low mowing weakens lawns severely. It is a bad habit to get into, and quite unnecessary. The difference between a healthy, often mowed lawn with a rich green hue and one that is regularly savaged leading to insipid colouring, is obvious.

The wrong grass may have been chosen for the site or conditions may have changed. You may have started off with an open, sunny garden and now that your trees are growing its whole aspect has changed. Areas under trees are not only shady but soil also tends to be dry and there is great root competition. Grass growing under trees must be cut very high indeed if it is to survive: 10cm (4in) is not

A PLEASANT SEATING area has been made here with a pergola on a paved area and the lawn lapping at the edges. Decorative grasses will not take much traffic, so seating areas are best placed on paving.

THIS LONG EXPANSE of lawn has been mown in alternating directions to give an impression of even greater length. The striped result also gives a pattern to what otherwise would have been a rather empty space between the two borders.

A FENCE TUMBLING with climbers here creates a partition between two distinct areas of a garden. This helps to effect a sense of space, as the visitor crosses from the paved seating area, busy with potted plants and flowering borders, to the open expanse of the lawn.

too high. Soil dryness and root competition may also lead to poor water penetration. This can happen on both sandy and clay-based soils. Use a commercial wetting agent on this area to ensure adequate moisture penetration—it should make quite a difference. If none of these measures are successful, you may need to put down another kind of grass in the problem area or consider growing groundcovers instead.

The area may have been subjected to heavy wear so that the soil has become compacted. Compacted soil results in poor root growth and also allows only poor water penetration. No grass, no matter how tough it is, can withstand constant traffic and still look good. There is simply no chance for it to recover. All you can do is try cutting the grass high and resign yourself to a thin or patchy lawn while the activity continues.

The lawn may have been killed with kindness. Lawns are sometimes made sparse by over-enthusiastic watering. In an attempt to have the perfect emerald green lawn some people just keep on watering and watering. You may get away with this if your lawn is on pure sand but otherwise soil becomes waterlogged and roots rot. A well-established home lawn should not need watering more often than once a week if that watering is a thorough soaking. In exceptionally high temperatures with drying winds it may be necessary to water twice a week.

Grass growth may also become poor and thin if soils become too acid. This is most often caused by regular use of sulphate of ammonia and some other high nitrogen fertilizers. Sulphate of ammonia does give a quick greening effect, but if you continue to use it by itself it can cause problems with the soil's acidity levels. Balanced lawn fertilizers certainly provide the nutrients needed by grass but if they are used several times in the growing season they can also contribute to soil acidity. To counteract this problem, simply give the lawn a dressing of lime once during the winter.

Aeration

In compacted or poorly aerated soils the root growth, and therefore grass growth, will be poor. To improve conditions you need to get the right balance of air and water in the soil. This may be done by using a coring machine, but in clay soils this may make conditions worse as the corer tends to smooth the sides and base of the hole, creating greater compaction.

It is better to use a garden fork pushed into the ground and worked back and forth in rows about 10cm (4in) apart. Then apply sand mixed with lime and brush it into the holes. Lime used at the rate of about 100g per sq/m (3oz per 10sq/ft) helps to flocculate the clay and thus improve aeration. Clay soils are best worked when they are just slightly damp. If the soil is too wet you will create more problems for yourself, as the holes fill in, and the whole project gets bogged down in mud – ultimately damaging your lawn. And if it is too dry the ground will be too hard to work – ultimately damaging your back!

Thatch

Thatch is a mat or layer of old runners that builds up under the top of the turf. It makes the lawn spongy and can inhibit the penetration of water, air and fertilizer, but it can be ignored unless you are after the perfect lawn.

Raking over the lawn on a regular basis during the growing season, especially after mowing, will help combat the problem. Little and often is the best policy to prevent any real build-up.

While it is quite easy to thatch a small garden by hand, using a spring-tined rake, larger lawns will need a powered machine. Always try and work across the lawn in different directions to remove every last shred of thatch. The lawn might look rather scruffy afterwards, but it quickly smoothes down again.

EDGING LAWNS

If you have a mower strip or well-spaded edges on your garden beds, edging will not be too much of a chore. Well-trimmed edges mean that grass will not spread into flower beds where it can quickly take over. Edges also create a general appearance of neatness. Note that grass tends to grow faster on the edges as there is generally no foot traffic there, and they often get more water than the rest of the lawn from overspray when watering garden beds. After trimming your lawn edges, rake or sweep up the clippings and add them to your compost heap.

Edging tools

There are several different kinds of edging tools readily available from garden centres. String line strimmers do a quick job but they should never be used to trim the grass around trees. There are many sad tales of trees that have been killed by being accidentally ring-barked with one of these tools—it is simply too late after the event. If you are using this kind of tool, make sure that you are wearing

THE EDGE *of this lawn takes on an organic shape, following the contours of the border closely, creating a relaxed yet formal air.*

strong boots and safety goggles to protect yourself, and don't allow children to play in the area until the job is complete.

On a firm surface beside a path a mechanical, long-handled edging tool does a very neat job. There are two types operated by hand, giving a choice of cutting head. One has a sharpened disc that rotates as it is pushed along, while the other has sharp-angled blades. A more expensive type has a petrol-driven motor. If the cutting edges of these tools are kept sharp, they are not difficult to use.

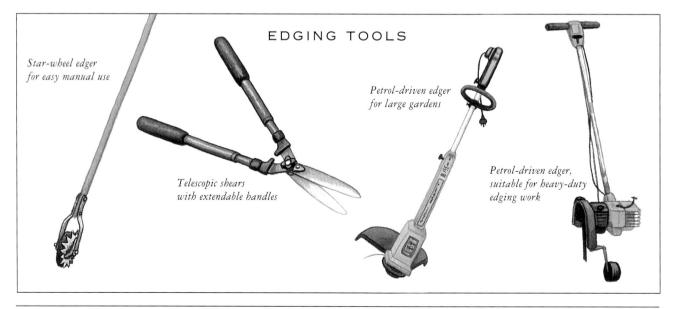

EDGING TOOLS

Star-wheel edger for easy manual use

Telescopic shears with extendable handles

Petrol-driven edger for large gardens

Petrol-driven edger, suitable for heavy-duty edging work

SOME AREAS JUST can't be turfed. Gravel has been used here in the place of grass. It creates the same sense of space as a lawn would, but has the added advantage of being able to have plants growing up through it. It also acts as a mulch – keeping weeds down and aiding drainage.

There are also some very satisfactory hand tools. Long-handled clippers are made with blades set at the vertical or horizontal. Vertically set blades are easiest to use along spaded edges of garden beds, while horizontally set blades may be easier to use against a mower strip or other firm edge. Both can be used from a standing position, an advantage for anyone who finds bending or kneeling difficult. For smaller lawns, or for gardeners who are happy to work on their hands and knees, there are cordless electric hand shears and the simple but effective shears.

Whichever tools you choose, make sure that you keep them clean and well sharpened. They will last twice as long, be easier to use and do the job well.

SPECIAL LAWN EQUIPMENT

Sprinklers

Lawn sprinklers range from sophisticated underground systems with pop-up heads and electronic timers to simple fixed, single head sprinklers. There are sprinklers with rotating heads and those that have a wide wave action. Your choice will be determined by the size of the lawn and the size of your wallet. When you are using a sprinkler keep checking that the water is soaking into the grass and not overspraying on to paths and drives, or simply running off and going to waste. You are likely to be using the sprinkler at times when rain is short, so be sure that there isn't a hose pipe ban in force before you start. You should also check water penetration by digging into the soil half an hour or so after you have turned off the sprinkler to see

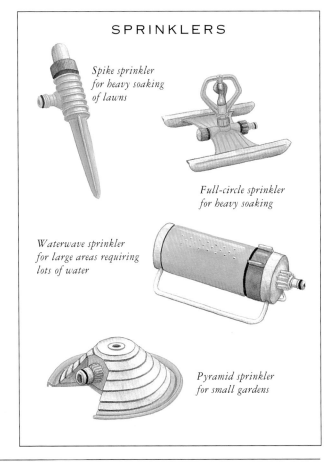

SPRINKLERS

Spike sprinkler for heavy soaking of lawns

Full-circle sprinkler for heavy soaking

Waterwave sprinkler for large areas requiring lots of water

Pyramid sprinkler for small gardens

MOWERS

Push lawn mower, suitable for small gardens and those who prefer manual tools

Engine-driven cylinder lawn mower with grass collector, for large or small jobs

Large rotary lawn mower with grass collector

Ride-on lawn mower for very large lawns

A RAMBLING GRAVEL PATH, invaded on all sides by border plants, carries the eye down to the oasis of a lush green lawn.

how far it has soaked into the ground. Garden centres and large hardware stores keep a wide range of sprinklers so that you can usually select the one that suits you best.

Rollers

Many people think that regular rolling will help to produce the perfect lawn. This is not necessarily so. When fresh turf is laid it is a good idea to roll it, especially if the area is large. Rolling newly laid turf ensures that there are no air pockets between the turf sod and the soil. It also provides good contact so that growing roots may penetrate well into the ground.

As a general maintenance procedure, however, rolling can actually be counter-productive. The only turf that can be rolled regularly without damage is turf growing on a well-formed, deep sand bed. Bowling greens and golf greens usually have this type of base, but very few home lawns are grown on a base prepared to this standard. Rolling lawns grown on average garden soils, and especially on clay-based soils, results in extreme soil compaction and greatly reduced aeration of the soil. This in turn leads to poor root growth and it may impede water penetration, too. The grass will soon show signs of stress.

Mowers

The lawn mower in most common use today is the rotary mower. Rotary mowers have horizontal cutting blades that revolve at high speed. The cutting height is adjustable and they are fairly easy to maintain. If the blades are kept well set and sharpened you get a good, satisfactory cut.

Mechanical cylinder mowers have the blades on a

turning cylinder that moves against a fixed base plate. There is also a roller behind the cutting cylinder. Cutting height is adjustable but they are more fiddly than rotary mowers and require more regular sharpening and maintenance. These mowers do, however, give a finer and much better finish to the lawn.

The hand cylinder mowers of today are lightweight and can be pushed with little effort. They are ideal for small, flattish lawn areas and are very simple to maintain. If the blades are kept sharpened they give a good finish to the lawn and can be used by almost anyone.

Ride-on mowers are used only on very large expanses of grass. They come in a range of sizes to suit everything from the large private lawn to huge parks. They are, of course, very expensive but are the only practical answer to very extensive lawn areas.

LAWN SUBSTITUTES

Grass lawns do not appeal to everyone and they involve a great deal of maintenance, but fortunately there are a number of substitutes with which to cover large areas.

Chamomile lawn

Chamomile (*Chamaemelum nobile*) is best known as a herb but it can also be grown as a lawn substitute. The fine, feathery, fragrant leaves and its creeping habit make a soft groundcover. It is not suitable for regular foot traffic but it can be walked on occasionally or sat on.

Chamomile flowers in summer (the flowers are used to make chamomile tea) and this may not suit everyone's idea of lawn. If it is mown to remove the flowers, a very high setting must be used on the mower to avoid damaging the plants. The non-flowering variety, 'Treneague', is the most suitable for lawn use and is readily available.

Chamomile is suitable for most climates and becomes dormant in winter. It prefers a sunny position and well-drained soil, and can be grown from seed sown in spring or by division of the roots of established plants. It is often grown in a small area surrounding a feature like a statue.

BULB PLANTS such as these snowdrops can be planted in a lawn to great effect. They lie dormant and invisible through the summer and winter, before bursting into life in the spring.

SAXIFRAGES form a dense matting of foliage and burst into flower in late winter.

LAWN CHAMOMILE looks charming and stepping stones avoid wear problems.

THYME, grown here on a raised bed, needs an open, sunny position to do well.

HOSTS OF DAFFODILS, as celebrated by Wordsworth, can be a triumphant seasonal highlight of a garden lawn. While not many of us have an entire field at our disposal for planting with bulbs, a colony of them in an area of the garden not frequently used will add a dash of colour.

Thyme lawn

Thyme (*Thymus*) is a perfect grass substitute for hot, dry areas. It is low growing and very fragrant, with very small, grey-green leaves. This useful plant spreads by means of creeping stems. It can also be used in the kitchen.

Thyme will not stand heavy wear but when walked on it releases its lovely aromatic fragrance. The pinkish-mauve flowers are very attractive to bees, and so summer, when they appear, is not a good time to walk on it!

NATURALIZING BULBS IN THE LAWN

Many bulbs will grow happily in grass where they can look delightfully natural. Traditionally, the bulbs used in this way have been snowflakes, snowdrops, crocus, daffodils and bluebells, but other bulbs can be used if they fit the picture you want.

The one disadvantage of growing bulbs in the lawn is that the grass cannot be mown for several months, until the foliage of the bulbs has died down naturally, otherwise the bulbs will be unlikely to flower the following year. However, this seasonal growth will not damage the lawn and it will help you to appreciate the freshly mowed turf when the time comes. This does mean, therefore, that small lawns or ones that are in general use are not suitable

THE ONLY DISADVANTAGE of planting bulbs is that the surrounding grass cannot be cut before flowers and foliage die off.

A CLASSIC LAWN AND BORDER arrangement. The neat edge of the lawn here acts as the first step of a stairway effect in the planting. The eye is then carried up to the medium-sized plants and then on up to the towering bank of roses at the rear of the bed.

for plantings of bulbs. If you do decide to try naturalizing bulbs in your lawn and still want to be able to use the body of the lawn, try to select an area that can be left unmown for several months, such as one on the perimeter of a lawn or adjacent to deciduous trees. On large estates bulb-planted lawns are usually set in an area of deciduous woodland or in a 'wild' garden, adding a dash of colour in areas that would normally be rather dull.

Planting the bulbs

If you are planting a large number of bulbs it may be worth investing in a bulb planting tool. This tool cuts down into the turf, removing a plug of grass and soil. Place the bulb in the bottom of the hole and then replace the plug. Alternatively, cut out a square of turf, plant a number of bulbs and then replace the cut turf. A good heavy watering should be given after planting to settle in the bulbs and help the cut turf to re-grow. Further watering should only be given if the weather is very dry and windy or the bulbs will rot. Once the bulbs have pushed out their first leaves, stop mowing and water only when the soil seems dry.

After flowering

Once the bulbs have bloomed and the flowers have faded, remove the spent flowers but leave the foliage to die down. Fertilize the bulbs with blood and bone or an all-purpose plant food and continue to water regularly until the

foliage starts to yellow and die off. This after-flowering treatment is most important as this is when the bulbs are storing their reserves for the following season's bloom.

Resume mowing once the foliage has died off. Keep the lawn cut high. This helps to shade and insulate the soil so that the dormant bulbs are not subject to extremes of temperature. It is also important not to overwater the area during summer as dormant bulbs are liable to rot when there is no leaf growth to transpire moisture.

DAFFODILS and grape hyacinth are planted in bold clumps to brighten this grassed area when the grass is still fairly dormant.

WHAT CAN GO WRONG?

WEEDS

Weeds should not be a big problem in well-established, well-maintained turf. Most serious weed problems result from low mowing, which weakens the grass, or occur in grass that has never established well because of shade or a poor choice of grass type. There should be few weed problems in new lawns if effective weed control measures have been taken when preparing the soil.

In newly laid turf, weeds are best removed by hand. For heavy weed infestation in established turf selective herbicides can be used, but before you buy a weedkiller read the label to check that it is suitable for your type of grass and that it will do the job. Read the fine print too, as a number of selective herbicides used on turf can damage the roots of trees and shrubs planted around the lawn. Even if a bad weed infestation has been allowed to develop, you can minimize weed spread by removing flower or seed heads before you mow.

Weeds to look out for
Many weeds thrive in lawns, if allowed. They can quickly spread and need to be tackled quite swiftly, before they take hold. Some are much more troublesome than others. You will quickly spot which have to be removed the moment you see them, and which (like buttercups, daisies and cow parsley) can be left in certain positions, making an attractive garden extra. The range of chemical treatments constantly changes, with new products regularly coming on the market. Note that some weeds will require more than one treatment.

The weeds are generally brought in by bird droppings containing seed, and by the wind. They fall into six main categories: thistles, plantains, etc., grasses, and moss.

Dandelions (*Taraxacum officinale*, *Hypochaeris radicata*)
Buttercups might be acceptable, but dandelions are one step too far. The real dandelion is *Taraxacum officinale* which has a long growing season from mid-spring to late autumn. The best way to remove it is chemically because getting the whole root out can be tricky and if any is left or

worse, sliced into tiny pieces, you end up with many more dandelions next year. *Hypochaeris radicata* is known as the cat's ear. It is very similar to a dandelion, with a slightly shorter growing season, and also has a long root that is tricky to get out by hand weeding. Treat chemically.

Dock (*Rumex*)
It appears in two forms, common and sheep's sorrel. The latter (*Rumex acetosella*) is by far the biggest nuisance and will produce tiny flowers if allowed. Spray or hand weed according to the severity of the infestation. The broad-leaved dock (*R. obtusifolius*) is a perennial with a deep root. It is more likely to occur in a border, and the whole plant with root needs to be carefully lifted out, making sure nothing is left behind.

Plantain (*Plantago* spp.)
The plantains are a nuisance, especially the broad-leaved kind (*Plantago major*). They regularly appear, and are quickly identified by their rosette-like, dull green, flat leaves about 10cm (4in) long, and vertical spikes with tiny flowers. If left they quickly despoil the lawn, looking very unsightly. The good news is that they are relatively easy to tackle. Spray or hand weed.

Thistle (*Cirsium* spp.)
It is a real pain but the good news is it is only likely to appear in old and neglected or brand new lawns. It can be quite quickly eradicated. The creeping thistle (*Cirsium arvense*) is immediately apparent with its spiky, fresh green leaves. If left it produces purple flowers. Treat chemically for instant success, though several mowings should also put an end to it.

Grasses
Look closely and, unless you have the finest top-quality lawn, there will be different kinds of grass that can become a problem. It is almost inevitable that some will appear at some time. Given the chance a few will spread and form significant tufts that really stand out. One of the worst offenders is *Holcus lanatus*.

The best way to tackle offending grasses is to make sure that the entire lawn is well cared for and well fed, so

that the invading kind cannot elbow aside the ones you want in the lawn. Grass weeds are best removed by digging them out, and then reseeding. You can spray with a chemical but you end up with a lawn covered with incredibly ugly, brownish-yellow spots. The problem will be most severe on new lawns.

Moss
Moss can be a nightmare. It can form small clumps, stick up, or run across the ground. Sadly, lawn owners have only themselves to blame for its appearance. Moss appears when conditions allow, and you will have to improve them to get rid of the problem. Treating with lawn sand is only a temporary solution.

Bad drainage is usually the chief cause. Compacted soil needs opening up with regular sessions using a large fork. The other cause is rapidly free-draining soil with few nutrients. Make sure that the lawn is well tended, well fed and well watered right through the growing season.

PESTS

Earthworms
Earthworms are normally the gardener's best friend but they can leave mounds of soil on the lawn surface, especially if the ground is wet. They do a great job aerating the soil but if you are a perfectionist and want to eradicate them, simply fertilize with sulphate of ammonia.

Ants
Ants make nests in dry areas. If your lawn is badly disrupted by ant nests you should treat the lawn with a commercial wetting agent, followed by a good, deep watering. This should remove the problem. Ants themselves are not a threat, just their nests.

Cats and dogs
Grass can be scorched by urine. If your own animals are the culprits, then regularly water the areas that they frequent. If neighbours' pets are making unwelcome visits then there are repellents available, based on aluminium ammonium sulphate or pepper dust, but these only provide temporary protection.

Slime mould
Slime mould is an unsightly but harmless lawn pest that can be removed by simply giving the the affected area a good watering down. The tiny creatures, varying in colour from white to orange, have characteristics of both animals and fungi. Common in early spring and early autumn, slime moulds release spores like fungi, and this tends to give the colony a greyish appearance.

Algae and gelatinous lichen
These charming micro-plants can form patches of green, grey or blackish slime on the surface of a lawn. Particularly unpleasant when trodden underfoot without shoes. They can be gotten rid of by making sure that the lawn is well drained and well aerated. Also prune back any overhanging trees or shrubs that may be creating the dark, dank conditions favoured by these pests

Dog lichen (*Peltigera canina*)
These small, leafy growths, greenish-black with pale yellow or cream lower sections, crop up in lawns that are in general poor condition. They can be removed using chemical measures and raking. To discourage their return, however, the lawn must be aerated and properly drained. Under the name of liverwort these lawn pests are actually valued and used in herbal medicine as a treatment for liver complaints.

Moles
These lovable stars of children's fiction can severely damage a well-kept lawn in a very short period of time. However, in utility lawns the occasional mole hill is not a serious problem. The presence of moles could even be said to be good for the lawn as they aerate the soil with their tunnels. But owners of high-quality lawns will neither welcome great mounds of earth appearing on the horizon, nor the subsidence that mole tunnels can create. The fresh earth exposed by mole hills also present the perfect planting site for any passing weeds. Moles can only be got rid of effectively by trapping (humane traps are available). Many other methods are on the market, such as mole smoke and ground shakers, but these are far from proven.

DISEASES

There's nothing worse than a well-loved and carefully nurtured lawn suddenly showing what look like alarming problems. The symptoms are invariably patches of yellow-brown grass. Tackle them quickly: once the lawn is weakened, weeds move in. The chief problems include:

Dollar spot (*Sclerotinia*)
This fungus (*Sclerotinia homeocarpa*) turns the grass pale brown, and generally occurs in damp spells in early autumn. High-quality lawns tend to be the worst sufferers. Treat with a fungicide. It also affects badly compacted ground which needs spiking to improve the drainage.

Fairy Rings
Look for a ring of dying grass with an outer ring of lush grass. The latter is highlighted by toadstools. In extreme cases there will be two rings of lush

ABOVE LEFT: Garden beds can look very effective when they are set into a large lawn. ABOVE: A path and wisteria arbour lead through this well-tended lawn.

grass, with dead grass between them. The cause is a fungus, and it forms a water-resistant covering that makes the grass wither and die of drought. Remedial action is clear. Do not waste any time on chemical cures, they do not work, but dig up the entire area to a minimum depth of 30cm (1ft) and remove. Also remove an area 30cm (1ft) beyond the outer ring. Make sure you do not leave any soil, debris or toadstools behind or the rings may well return.

Red Thread (*Corticium fuciforme*)
Quality lawns with plenty of fescues are most likely to suffer from red thread. Falling nitrogen levels through lack of feeding and poor aeration can also lead to an outbreak. An infestation of this fungal growth leads to circular or irregular bleached or reddish patches on a lawn. On close examination you will be able to see small, red, thread-like structures on the tips of the infected blades of grass. This fungus appears in cool, moist weather. The problem is easily tackled with a high nitrogen lawn feed and spiking.

Snow Mould
Of all the lawn diseases, this is the most likely to strike. Small patches of grass turn brownish-yellow and start to join up. Look out for it in the autumn, and in mild winters. Treat with a fungicide and by spiking the lawn to improve aeration.

THE SEED SELECTOR

HIGH-QUALITY LAWNS

Remember that when re-grassing bare patches on an existing lawn, you should use the same kind of seed. Areas of high-quality grass will stand out for years in an old lawn with daisies and buttercups. New supergrasses will also outgrow the rest of the lawn. Also note that a top-quality lawn will consist of a mix of the following seeds.

Browntop bent (*Agrostis tenuis*)
This is a low-growing tufted grass with short rhizomes. It can be slow to take off, but soon creates an excellent sward. It withstands regular close cropping, and even dry spells. It is equally happy growing in acid soil as in alkaline. Browntop is used in most quality seed grass mixes.

Highland bent (*Agrostis castellana*)
Like Browntop, this gives first-rate results. Seed can either be bought in separate batches, enabling you to make up your own mix, or in ready-made bags.

Fescue (*Festuca rubra* var. *commutata*)
Fescues are a key part of any high-quality mix, and this one adds a dense tuft, and an ability to withstand close mowing. It even grows in rather dry soils.

Creeping red fescue (*Festuca rubra* var. *rubra*)
By itself this would not produce the best lawn because it can be rather lax. It needs to be bulked up with other first-rate kinds of grass seed. It is good at withstanding dry, even sandy soil, but does not perform that well when close mowed on a regular basis.

UTILITY LAWNS

Note that an all-purpose lawn usually consists of rye grass mixed with creeping red fescue, smooth-stalked meadow grass, and bent.

Smooth-stalked meadow grass (*Poa pratensis*)
This grass can take a while to get established, but thereafter it quickly spreads and tends to look after itself well. It is good in dry conditions, and withstands plenty of foot traffic. This grass also tolerates a fairly wide range of soils, except extreme conditions, but is best on light, free-draining soil. In general, it is a safe bet for a lawn that might not receive much in the way of love and attention, and has to put up with children's games.

Rye grass (*Lolium perenne*)
This is the mainstay of most all-purpose garden mixes. It quickly takes and is hard-wearing. While it grows in virtually all garden soils, it does prefer some moisture through the growing season and is best suited to parts of the garden that do not rapidly dry out. New varieties of perennial rye grass have improved the utility lawn, making it much more hard-wearing and better looking.

BELOW: With rambling beds spilling into it from all sides, this lawn flows like a river through the various area of the garden. The plantings use the various shades of green in the foliage to great effect, creating dappled areas of light and dark. Occasional areas of flowers, restrained to heighten their impact, are spotted around the edges of the lawn. The house itself is nearly invisible in the background.

QUALITY GRASSES

AGROSTIS TENUIS, A. PALUSTRIS

Browntop bent, creeping bent

BROWNTOP AND CREEPING BENT are often grown together to produce a lawn with a very fine finish.

FEATURES

Fine-leaved

Browntop bent (*A. tenuis*) and creeping bent (*A. palustris*) make very even, fine lawns suitable for cool, humid regions but they are very high maintenance grasses. Browntop bent is a tufted grass more suitable for home lawns than creeping bent, which has a high growth rate and needs a great deal of water and fertiliser. Both bent grasses are used on bowling greens and golf greens because of the high quality, fine-textured turf. There are several cultivars available.

FESTUCA RUBRA VAR. COMMUTATA

Chewings fescue

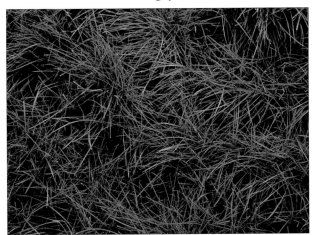

ALTHOUGH OFTEN USED in blends, Chewings fescue can form a good, dense lawn on its own. It is fairly drought resistant.

FEATURES

Fine-leaved

This is a fine, dark green, tufted grass which forms a dense lawn. It is often used in mixtures with Kentucky blue grass to make a very good quality lawn blend. It can be grown under trees as long as it is cut high, and although it is not suitable for high-wear areas it does tolerate normal domestic traffic – but not football matches! It is a good all-purpose lawn for cool areas. Growth is extremely slow in winter but it becomes completely dormant only if it is very cold.

UTILITY LAWNS

LOLIUM MULTIFLORUM, L. PERENNE

Rye grass

MOSTLY USED in grass mixtures, rye is quick to establish, a great advantage in new gardens and where lawns have to be hard-wearing.

FEATURES

Fine-leaved

Annual (*L. multiflorum*) and perennial (*L. perenne*) rye grasses are rarely used on their own as they do not give good results, but are often included in general seed mixtures where quick cover is wanted. They are frequently used on home lawns, parklands and golf fairways. Because they have the ability to establish themselves particularly rapidly, these grasses are also used on banks where erosion control is required. These tufted grasses are generally not suitable for lawns where a 'bowling green' finish is required. This is because they do not mow particularly evenly. However, they are soft to sit and walk on, and cut down to a pleasant, mat-like surface. These grasses relish cool climates, and present few problems for the gardener.

GROWING GROUND-COVER

Groundcover gives the finishing touches to the garden—it could be described as a living carpet. By covering the ground between shrubs and other plantings, groundcover creates a soft, natural look. In nature there is always something growing on the ground under trees and shrubs except where there is very deep leaf litter or very low light levels.

Groundcover has practical aspects, too. Once it is established it can suppress weeds and has a natural mulching effect on the soil, helping to maintain a fairly even temperature and moisture level around the roots of larger plants. It is ideal in low-maintenance gardens and as grass substitutes in heavy shade under trees or on sloping ground that is too difficult to mow. Groundcover can also be used to hold soil on steep sites, thus helping to prevent erosion, and as cover on landfill or very poor soil.

LEFT: In full flower, snow-in-summer is as pretty a groundcover as you could wish for. Flowers almost obscure the foliage and give added height to the planting during the blooming period. When blooming is over, a quick shear reveals the neat, silvery leaves. The pretty tree on the right is a standard weeping mulberry.

A PLEASANT EFFECT is produced by this Vinca major, *growing at the base of a tree. Groundcover plants can frequently be used to add colour and texture to an area where other plants could not grow.* V. major *in particular will grow well in shaded areas.*

CHOOSING A GROUNDCOVER

Groundcover comes in a variety of different forms. There are plants that spread by runners, such as blue bugle flower, and trailing plants. Mat-forming plants such as baby's tears and thrift are excellent groundcovers, as are those that spread by horizontal growth. Climbing plants such as ivy can also be used successfully as groundcovers.

As with any other type of plant, it is important to choose the right groundcover for the aspect, climate, soil and space available. Some groundcover plants are suitable for sunny spots but some prefer shade. Growing a plant in the wrong place will lead to disappointment. Some groundcover plants, such as *Viola hederacea*, can be very vigorous, and need constant control if planted for a small space. Other mat-forming plants, such as *Armeria maritima* (sea thrift), are more sedate and easy to confine.

PLANTING

Most groundcovers are long-term plantings and so it is worth putting some effort into good soil preparation and weeding. Since the new plantings may have to compete against established trees or shrubs, it is a good idea to give them plenty of food by digging in some well-decayed manure or compost a few weeks before planting.

Weed eradication is important as it is frustrating to find weeds coming up through groundcover. Most weeds will not be eliminated in one go. Dig out any you can see or spot-spray them with glyphosate. Once they have gone or are dead, fork over the soil again, water it and wait for the next crop of weeds to emerge. This reduces the bank of weed seeds lying dormant in the ground. Perennial weeds such as oxalis will need a determined effort to get rid of.

Spacing plants

When you are planting groundcover, space the individual plants out carefully to achieve the desired result. If you need to cover an area quickly, space the plants closer together, but remember to make allowance for the final size of the plants. A large grower such as rosemary may be spaced at 1m (3ft) intervals or for quicker cover at 45cm (18in) spacings. A smaller, clumping plant such as

WHAT CAN GO WRONG?

The different kinds of groundcover described in the following entries are all remarkably free of pest and disease problems. Any specific problems related to each plant are discussed under the plant entry. Groundcover plants tend to take care of themselves, as long as they are given favourable aspects and soil conditions.

THESE DIFFERENT-COLOURED ericas have formed a sea of colour on this slope. Their tiny flowers create a pleasing texture.

CREATING A PATCHWORK effect, these rosemarys are not just groundcover, but also plants that add colour and scent to the garden.

lamb's ears could be planted at spacings of 23cm (9in) for quick cover or as far apart as 1m (3ft). If covering a large area of ground, zigzag the plantings to ensure good final cover. Mulch the areas of bare soil between the plants while you wait for them to grow.

MAINTENANCE

The ultimate spread of a groundcover will depend on the type of plant, the soil conditions and the care it receives. Most groundcovering plants need regular feeding during the growing season because of the intense root competition that will occur if they are planted under trees and shrubs. Regular watering is also needed, especially in the early stages of establishment. And remember to keep any bare areas between plants mulched to prevent weeds establishing themselves.

Controlling growth

Once the plants have become established, they need little maintenance beyond shearing off spent flower stems or trimming to confine them to a specific area. They are often quite hardy plants whose rambling habit of growth makes them tough and resistant to extremes of weather.

Some plants need time and trouble spent to get them established, but thereafter they will virtually look after themselves. They may still need occasional trimming along the edges to keep them under control.

Plants such as blue bugle flower can become very dense and congested. This ultimately means that the growth may end up not looking very attractive. If this happens, it is usually easy to pull out some of the excess growth throughout the area, or to lift and divide whole sections of the planting. Replant younger looking growths and discard the old ones.

If any sections of your groundcover have died out altogether, dig them out and replace them with fresh plants from the edges of the planting or lift and divide healthy, vigorous growths. If it is not the kind of plant that can be lifted and divided, look for any pieces that have rooted down or take fresh cuttings.

It is very tempting to plant up an area with groundcover and then forget about it and leave it alone. But it is well worth the occasional check. Growth might be more rampant in one spot than another and need to be evened out, or there might be the odd bare patch. Groundcover invariably spills out of its allotted space and heads towards an area with ornamental plantings. Without a regular look you may suddenly find that your ornamental bed is losing its shape and being taken over. Be ruthless. Cut back the groundcover with a spade.

USING GROUNDCOVERS IN ROCKERIES

Many groundcover plants are also suitable for use as rockery plants, but as always it is essential to choose the right plant for the particular situation. For a small rockery, you should try to choose plants that will not outgrow their allotted space too soon, but for very large rockeries you may have enough room for more spreading or trailing groundcover. Plants used in rockeries should not need a constantly moist soil, as the soil in rockeries tends to dry out fairly quickly.

A ROLLING CARPET of purple erica transforms what would otherwise be a rather plain area. Taking up large areas of the garden, groundcover suppresses weeds and requires very little in the way of maintentance. The fact that erica is pleasing to the eye is an added bonus.

Establishing a rockery

A rockery is usually best sited on sloping ground where it looks natural and rocks can be partly bedded securely into the ground. This also means that drainage is fairly rapid, therefore suiting plants that like dry conditions.

Choose rock that occurs naturally in the area as this will blend in better with the site, but never remove rocks from the countryside. This is very destructive to the environment as the rock, once removed, cannot be replaced. In most areas rock should be available from building excavations. If the rock looks too raw, mix some cow manure and water to a thin slurry and paint it over the rock—this will hasten the weathered look and encourage the growth of lichens and mosses.

Rock gardens are fairly high maintenance areas, at least in their early years, and so it is important to remove perennial weeds and grasses from the area before planting. Once the rockery has been planted it is extremely difficult to get rid of more persistent weeds with long, deep tap roots. Any pieces of root not removed can produce new plants. Roots of trees adjacent to the area may also invade the rockery once the soil has been loosened and new plants are being watered and fed regularly.

Selecting plants

A rockery doesn't have to have a different kind of plant in every available pocket—in fact, that could result in a very 'spotty' effect. Aim for harmony of colour or repeat the same plant in different parts of the rockery. For instance, if you are using a grey-foliaged plant, it may look better to place two or three together in different parts of the planting. A very attractive display may even be made using only one type of plant in many colours. An exception to this would be a rockery planted with a collection of true alpine plants, many of which are miniature treasures grown by an avid collector who wishes to try as many different types as possible.

NATIVE VIOLETS can become a little invasive but they make a top groundcover for their ease of culture and long flowering.

AN EYE-CATCHING FEATURE has been made of this Common ivy encircling a tiny pond. Ivy is a good groundcover under trees.

AJUGA REPTANS
Blue bugle flower

THE FLOWER SPIKES of Ajuga reptans *sit up above the rosettes of foliage. Their colour varies with the variety and exposure to the sun.*

SOME VARIETIES of A. reptans *produce pink and cream tones. To retain their colour, they need more sun than the plain species.*

FEATURES

Partial Shade

A lovely groundcover for shady, slightly moist sites, *Ajuga reptans* grows as a neat rosette of leaves but spreads by stolons (running stems). Leaves are shiny and may be dark green or bronzed green. The cultivars 'Burgundy Lace' and 'Multicolor' are mottled cream, pink or burgundy. This long-lived plant rarely grows more than 15cm (6in) high, although the deep blue flower spikes may be taller. It is an ideal groundcover under trees and is a good soil binder. It is also used as a border plant and can be grown in troughs or pots. Once the plant is established, growth is dense so that it suppresses weeds very well.

CONDITIONS

Aspect   A woodland and hedgerow plant, *A. reptans* prefers shade or dappled sunlight.

AJUGA AT A GLANCE

Ajuga reptans is a quality groundcover plant, with excellent coloured forms for the late spring garden. Hardy to −15°C (5°F).

		RECOMMENDED VARIETIES
JAN	foliage	*Ajuga reptans*
FEB	foliage	A. r. 'Braunherz'
MAR	foliage	A. r. 'Burgundy Glow'
APRIL	foliage	A. r. 'Catlin's Giant'
MAY	flowering	A. r. 'Multicolor'
JUNE	flowering	A. r. 'Tricolor'
JULY	foliage	A. r. 'Variegata'
AUG	foliage	
SEPT	foliage	
OCT	foliage	
NOV	foliage	
DEC	foliage	

Site   This plant does best in well-drained, but somewhat moisture-retentive soil that has been enriched with plenty of organic matter prior to planting. It can also sometimes occur in surprisingly boggy places.

GROWING METHOD

Propagation   Best grown from divisions of existing clumps, *A. reptans* roots easily from stem nodes and any small sections that are dug up will rapidly re-establish.

Feeding   Feed with an application of blood and bone, pellets of poultry manure or any complete plant food after flowering.

Problems   *A. reptans* can be badly affected by powdery mildew if air circulation is poor or the soil is badly drained. If the weather is not too hot, sulphur dust or spray can suppress this mildew. Otherwise use a fungicide registered for powdery mildew.

FLOWERING

Season   The attractive bright blue flower spikes are produced in spring, or in the early summer in cool areas. They make a lovely garden display. 'Variegata' is probably the best form with its highly-decorative white edged leaves. It is not that reliable though and needs close attention. 'Braunherz' has a remarkably rich bronze colour.

Cutting   The flowers of *A. reptans* are good as cut flowers.

PRUNING

General   Pruning should be restricted to the removal of the spent flower stems.

ALCHEMILLA MOLLIS
Lady's mantle

LIME-GREEN FLOWERS light up Alchemilla mollis. *Although it is not a particularly bright colour, it lifts the whole area.*

THIS MASSED PLANTING of A. mollis *behind a dwarf box hedge will defy any competition from weeds or other plants.*

FEATURES

Sun or
Part Shade

Alchemilla mollis is a quick-growing, herbaceous perennial that is mostly used along the edges of paths or borders. It is effective for suppressing weeds and sows itself freely, often popping up in cracks in paths or paving. Growing to anything up to 60cm (2ft) high, one plant may spread to 75cm (30in). The rounded, slightly hairy leaves overlap one another and it produces trusses of bright lime-green flowers through summer. It provides a lovely contrast with other strong colours.

ALCHEMILLA AT A GLANCE

A. mollis is an essential self-seeding perennial for cottage gardens that can form incredible groundcover. Hardy to −18°C (0°F).

		COMPANION PLANTS
JAN	/	Cotoneaster
FEB	/	Elaeagnus
MAR	/	Fuchsia
APRIL	foliage 🍂	Hebe
MAY	foliage 🍂	Holly
JUNE	flowering ✽	Lavender
JULY	flowering ✽	Pittosporum
AUG	flowering ✽	Rose
SEPT	flowering ✽	
OCT	foliage 🍂	
NOV	foliage 🍂	
DEC	foliage 🍂	

CONDITIONS

Aspect
The more sun it receives the better, where you can also see the morning dew on the foliage. It is a willing performer, a sure spreader, and also grows well in light shade.

Site
Needs to be grown in well-drained soil with a high organic content.

GROWING METHOD

Propagation
Self-sown seedlings can easily be transplanted to other positions. Clumps can be divided in either autumn or spring.

Feeding
Apply blood and bone or complete plant food in spring as new growth begins.

Problems
No specific problems are known.

FLOWERING

Season
Masses of lime-green flowers appear throughout summer.

Cutting
Flowers are popular with flower arrangers.

PRUNING

General
Shear the whole plant back hard in midsummer and you get a fresh surge of new lime green foliage and flowers. Otherwise it takes care of itself.

ANEMONE
Windflower

BETWEEN THEM, the anemones have just about all the colours of the rainbow, with various shades of red, pink, mauve, blue and yellow. There are species, such as Anemone ranunculoides, *that enjoy a partially shaded position and are therefore perfect for woodland areas of the garden.*

FEATURES

Shade or
Part Shade

Anemones are a large genus with lots of excellent woodland plants like *Anemone ranunculoides*. It is a spreading perennial growing about 10cm (4in) high, and 45cm (18in) wide, with yellow flowers in spring. Other good woodland-type anenomes include the white *A. nemorosa*, slightly shorter and it does not spread quite as far. Most of the other anenomes are more strikingly obvious, like the dark pink *A. hupehensis* which grows 60cm (2ft) high or more. The Japanese anemone, *A. hupehensis japonica*, has striking white flowers. It lasts well into autumn.

ANEMONE AT A GLANCE

Anemone ranunculoides is a spring-flowering, short woodland plant with a good spread. There is a double form. Hardy to –15°C (5°F).

		RECOMMENDED VARIETIES
JAN	/	*Anemone blanda*
FEB	/	*A. blanda* 'Radar'
MAR	/	*A. blanda* 'White Star'
APRIL	foliage 🌿	*A. hupehensis*
MAY	flowering ❀	*A. hupehensis* 'Hadspen
JUNE	foliage 🌿	Abundance'
JULY	foliage 🌿	*A. hupehensis* 'Bressingham
AUG	foliage 🌿	Glow'
SEPT	foliage 🌿	*A.* x *hybrida* 'Honorine
OCT	/	Jobert'
NOV	/	*A. ranunculoides*
DEC	/	

CONDITIONS

Aspect *Anemone ranunculoides* needs a rather shady position, as if growing in an open woodland. Some shade during the day is necessary.

Site The soil should be dampish, and definitely not hot, dry and free-draining. Adding well-rotted organic matter should aid moisture retention, and improve and feed the soil.

GROWING METHOD

Propagation Divide the rhizomes in the spring, or in the autumn when the leaves have dropped. One mature plant should yield plenty of new vigorous plants.

Feeding Apply a slow-release fertilizer in the spring. This should ensure a spectacular flower display through the season.

Problems The most typical problem comes from hungry slugs. They can ruin the foliage and new shoots. Spreading sharp sand or gravel round the plants keeps slugs away.

FLOWERING

Season *A. ranunculoides* flowers in the spring.

Cutting It makes good cut flowers.

PRUNING

General No pruning is necessary.

ANTHEMIS TINCTORIA
Ox-eye chamomile

THE YELLOW FLOWERS of Anthemis tinctoria *light up the garden on the greyest day, contrasting well with the dark foliage.*

THE LONG FLOWERING PERIOD, pretty foliage and ease of maintenance make A. tinctoria *a good choice for busy gardeners.*

FEATURES

Full Sun

With ferny foliage and bright yellow daisy flowers, *Anthemis tinctoria* makes a striking and easy-care groundcover. The plant may grow up to 90cm (3ft) high and spread by the same amount. The floral display is long lasting: it should be around through late spring and summer. There are a number of named cultivars available. This is a vigorous plant that may sometimes need restraining, although it never gets totally out of hand. Ox-eye chamomile plants need renewing every two or three years but they are easy to propagate. An alternative common name for this plant is dyer's chamomile, because the flowers yield a distinctive yellow dye.

ANTHEMIS AT A GLANCE

Anthemis tinctoria gives both decent cover and a fine array of yellow flowers at the height of summer. Hardy to –18°C (0°F).

		RECOMMENDED VARIETIES
JAN	/	*Anthemis* 'Grallagh Gold'
FEB	/	*A. punctata cupaniana*
MAR	/	*A. tinctoria*
APRIL	/	*A. tinctoria* 'Alba'
MAY	foliage ❧	*A tinctoria* 'E. C. Buxton'
JUNE	flowering ✽	*A. tinctoria* 'Kelwayi'
JULY	flowering ✽	*A. tinctoria* 'Sauce
AUG	flowering ✽	Hollandaise'
SEPT	foliage ❧	*A. tinctoria* 'Wargrave
OCT	foliage ❧	Variety'
NOV	/	
DEC	/	

CONDITIONS

Aspect   Must have full sun all day for best flowering. Keep it well out of the shade.

Site   Soil should be well drained but need not be rich. *A. tinctoria* will tolerate quite poor soil.

GROWING CONDITIONS

Propagation   The one big problem with *A. tinctoria* is that it has quite a short shelf-life. Either prune (see below) or regularly grow new young plants from divisions. Divide plants in the spring or the autumn, making sure each section has good roots. You can also increase your stock by taking cuttings in the spring.

Feeding   Fertilize lightly with blood and bone, poultry manure or complete plant food in early spring.

Problems   No specific problems are known.

FLOWERING

Season   Flowering right through the summer.

Cutting   Flowers can be picked for posies.

PRUNING

General   Prune flowers as they fade to prolong blooming. This also forces plants to develop new strong growths which prolong their lifespan. Also note that plants can be cut back at any time during the growing season if they need restricting.

ARABIS CAUCASICA
Rock cress

THIS DOUBLE WHITE FORM of rock cress closely resembles its relative, the stock. The light fragrance is reminiscent of stock too.

A GENEROUS DRIFT of rock cress fills a section of this perennial border, which is edged with low-growing, pink alpine phlox.

FEATURES

Full Sun

Of the many species of rock cress, this is probably the most commonly grown. It spreads to form mats of leafy rosettes and will grow to around 15cm (6in) high. This vigorous plant may spread to 30cm (1ft). It can be grown in rockeries, between paving stones or as a border plant. Flowers are produced over a long season from late winter into summer. They are white in the species but there is a pink form and also a double white variety, 'Flore Pleno'. There are a number of other named cultivars. *Arabis caucasica* is related to stock as is obvious from the flowers, and it has the fragrance associated with stocks.

ARABIS AT A GLANCE

Arabis caucasica is a fun, white-flowering evergreen perennial best grown in walls. It can be quite invasive. Hardy to −18°C (0°F).

JAN	foliage	
FEB	foliage	
MAR	foliage	
APRIL	foliage	
MAY	flowering	
JUNE	foliage	
JULY	foliage	
AUG	foliage	
SEPT	foliage	
OCT	foliage	
NOV	foliage	
DEC	foliage	

RECOMMENDED VARIETIES
Arabis x *arendsii* 'Rosabella'
A. blepharophylla
 'Fruhlingszauber'
A. bryoides
A. caucasica 'Flore Pleno'
A. caucasica 'Variegata'
A. procurrens 'Variegata'

CONDITIONS

Aspect Needs full sun.
Site Soil must be very well drained but need not be rich. Add lime or dolomite to very acid soils before planting. Heavy soils must be broken up with sharp grit and sand.

GROWING METHOD

Propagation Make divisions of an existing clump in autumn or spring. Generally, though, it is often easier to leave plants where they are and then to propagate from cuttings taken in the summer.
Feeding Apply a light dressing of complete plant food in spring.
Problems Avoid overwatering and make sure these plants are situated where air circulation is good. Plants can collapse in warm, moist conditions but this is extremely unlikely to occur in our climate.

FLOWERING

Season The brief but eyecatching display happens in spring with the warm weather.
Cutting Flowers can be picked for posies if the stems are long enough.

PRUNING

General Can be cut back hard once after blooming.

ARMERIA MARITIMA
Sea thrift

ARMERIA MARITIMA *IS known as 'sea pink' in its natural habitat where it forms dense mounds on exposed sea cliffs.*

A GENEROUS PLANTING of A. maritima *fills a sunny corner by an old wall. Dainty little erigeron creeps out from under the thrift.*

FEATURES

Full Sun

Also known as 'sea pink', this small, tufted plant makes mounded cushions of foliage. Established growth is very dense. Flowers, which may be pink, white or nearly red, stand above the foliage on stems that reach up to 20cm (8in) or more. There are a number of named cultivars available. *Armeria maritima* has a long flowering period provided spent flowers are removed regularly. It is mostly used as an edging plant or grown in rockeries but it can be grown in containers too.

CONDITIONS

Aspect Needs an open, sunny position; tolerates exposed, windy coastal conditions extremely

Site well, hence its name, though it is also found growing in mountains.
Soil must be very well drained but it need not be rich. Do not risk growing it on heavy wet soils, where its roots will rot the first winter and die.

GROWING METHOD

Propagation Grows best from divisions of an existing clump, which should be broken up and replanted during the first part of spring.

Feeding Apply little or no fertilizer as this may stimulate lush foliage growth, which is prone to problems. If the soil is very poor, feed lightly with some complete plant food during early spring. A slow-release fertiliser is best, rather than a sudden quick-fix application.

Problems Rust, a fungal disease, can be a problem in very humid conditions – spray with a registered fungicide. Overwatering and poor drainage will cause plants to collapse.

FLOWERING

Season The pink, white or red flowers will appear from spring through summer if spent flowers are removed regularly.

Cutting Flowers can be cut for the vase or spent blooms simply cut off.

PRUNING

General Remove spent flowers. Deadheading prolongs flowering.

ARMERIA AT A GLANCE

Armeria maritima is the indispensable perennial for seaside gardens, where it adds good spring, and summer colour. Hardy to –18°C (0°F).

		RECOMMENDED VARIETIES
JAN	/	*Armeria alliacea*
FEB	/	'Bees Ruby'
MAR	/	*A. juniperifolia*
APRIL	foliage	*A. juniperifolia* 'Bevan's Variety'
MAY	foliage	
JUNE	flowering	*A. maritima*
JULY	foliage	*A. maritima* 'Bloodstone'
AUG	foliage	*A. maritima* 'Vindictive'
SEPT	foliage	*A. pseudarmeria*
OCT	/	
NOV	/	
DEC	/	

BALLOTA
Ballota

THE PLEASANT SCALLOPED foliage of Ballota pseudodictamnus *creates a variegated effect as the lighter-coloured undersides of the leaves curls up and catch the sunlight. The downy texture of these plants also provides an attractive contrast of texture with glossier, darker green foliage.*

FEATURES

Full Sun

Ballota pseudodictamnus is a mound-forming evergreen sub-shrub, growing about 45cm (18in) high, and spreading to about 60cm (2ft). It has an abundance of rounded leaves covered with silvery grey wool. It needs very little care beyond a spring prune, and its whitish flowers appear from spring into early summer. It thrives best in full sun and, like the other ballotas commonly available, is not quite fully hardy. *B. acetabulosa* is slightly bushier and taller, making a more dominant plant. Neither belong to the first division of shrubs, but they are good at covering bare patches of soil. They can be pruned giving a shorter height, emphasizing the spread.

BALLOTA AT A GLANCE

Ballota pseudodictamnus has all-year woolly leaves, and white flowers with a pink tinge in spring and early summer. Hardy to –5°C (23°F).

JAN	foliage 🌿	RECOMMENDED VARIETIES
FEB	foliage 🌿	*Ballota* 'All Hallows Green'
MAR	foliage 🌿	*B. nigra*
APRIL	flowering ❀	*B. n.* 'Archer's Variegated'
MAY	flowering ❀	*B. acetabulosa*
JUNE	flowering ❀	*B. pseudodictamnus*
JULY	foliage 🌿	
AUG	foliage 🌿	
SEPT	foliage 🌿	
OCT	foliage 🌿	
NOV	foliage 🌿	
DEC	foliage 🌿	

CONDITIONS

Aspect   Full sun or sun for most of the day is the key to success with these plants. Keep them away from the shade.

Site   Completely avoid any soil that has been enriched. Ballotas will flourish in soils other plants would consider poor. It should also be quite light and free draining.

GROWING METHOD

Propagation   The best and cheapest method for propagation is to take dozens of cuttings in the early part of summer. They quickly take but do need protection through the cold winter months. Plant out the following spring when they are well hardened off.

Feeding   This is one occasion when feeding of any description is really not necessary.

Problems   Ballotas are remarkably trouble free. The plants take care of themselves.

FLOWERING

Season   The small white flowers with a pink tinge appear through late spring, and the first part of summer. In the case of *B. acetabulosa* they appear in the middle and end part of summer.

PRUNING

General   A spring prune produces plenty of fresh new growth and keeps it in good shape.

BERGENIA CILIATA

Elephant's ears

THE LARGE LEAVES *of bergenias lead to their popular name of elephant's ears. This foliage makes them prime groundcover plants.*

PROVIDING A WELCOME *lift to the garden in the winter, the blooms of* Bergenia ciliata *bob amid a sea of lush green foliage.*

FEATURES

Shade or Part Shade

Bergenias make excellent evergreen groundcover plants. They are also known as elephant's ears because of the large, rounded leaves about 20–30cm (8–12in) long. They are often leathery and glossy, generally green, many turning reddish in the autumn. The flowers are held on short stems from mid-spring to early summer. *Bergenia ciliata* has pink flowers and tends to lose its foliage in cold winters. It should survive most winters but in very bad freezing spells it may succumb, and should be protected. It grows about 30cm (1ft) high, and 45cm (18in) wide. Like all bergenias it is generally long living and easy to propagate. It is a useful plant, able to colonize areas other plants can't reach, such as beneath trees. It can also be used at the front of a border, or even to line the edge of paths.

BERGENIA AT A GLANCE

Bergenia ciliata is a large-leaved, pink flowering perennial that thrives in a wide range of conditions. Hardy to −15°C (5°F).

		RECOMMENDED VARIETIES
JAN	/	*Bergenia* 'Adenglut'
FEB	/	B. 'Baby Doll'
MAR	flowering ❃	B. 'Bressingham Salmon'
APRIL	flowering ❃	B. 'Bressingham White'
MAY	foliage	B. *ciliata*
JUNE	foliage	B. *cordifolia* 'Purpurea'
JULY	foliage	B. *c.* 'Morgenrote'
AUG	foliage	B. *purpurascens*
SEPT	foliage	B. *p.* 'Silberlicht'
OCT	/	
NOV	/	
DEC	/	

CONDITIONS

Aspect   It grows in either full sun or shady areas, but avoid extremes of the latter.

Site   Likes well composted, moist soil with good drainage. It will tolerate much poorer conditions that bring out a richer leaf colour in winter.

GROWING METHOD

Propagation   Grow from seeds sown in the spring to produce hybrids, or divide in the spring or autumn every five years or so. This will rejuvenate a declining plant. Place up to 60cm (2ft) apart, depending on the variety, or closer for immediate coverage.

Feeding   Feed generously in early spring with a complete plant food, especially on poorer ground, and give a generous layer of mulch both in the spring, and again in the autumn.

Problems   Slugs and snails can be a major problem to the young foliage, ruining its shapely appearance. Pick off, or attack with chemicals. Spray with a fungicide if leaf spot occurs.

FLOWERING

Season   The flowers appear from late winter or early spring, depending on variety, for a few weeks.

Cutting   Though the flowers are useful in cut flower arrangements, the foliage, especially when red in winter, makes a particularly attractive foil.

PRUNING

General   Remove the spent flower stem and foliage.

CALLUNA VULGARIS

Heather

A MASSED PLANTING of Culluna vulgaris 'Firefly' creates a rippling sea of magenta, as the blooms emerge.

HEATHER CAN BE a spectacular display plant, as this group demonstrates. The variety of colours creates a stunning patchwork effect.

FEATURES

Full Sun

The heathers are evergreen shrubs that demand acid soil. There is just one species with scores of excellent cultivars. The best way to choose between them is to visit special heather gardens and nurseries, buying forms that make a fun 'patchwork quilt'. Many have coloured foliage with red, purple, bronze, grey and gold, and many green-leaved ones change colour come the autumn. The key difference between heathers and ericas is that the latter include varieties that flower in late winter/spring, while heathers peak from midsummer to autumn. Most heathers spread about 45cm (18in). Some have flowers that contrast with and stand out against the foliage. One such is the cultivar 'Firefly', with magenta flowers and beige leaves.

CALLUNA AT A GLANCE

Heathers are vital components of the winter garden, valued for their wide range of attractively coloured foliage. Hardy to −18°C (0°F).

JAN	foliage 🌿	RECOMMENDED VARIETIES
FEB	foliage 🌿	*Calluna vulgaris*
MAR	foliage 🌿	C. v. 'Allegro'
APRIL	foliage 🌿	C. v. 'Beoley Gold'
MAY	foliage 🌿	C. v. 'Blazeaway'
JUNE	foliage 🌿	C. v. 'Elsie Purnell'
JULY	flowering ✳	C. v. 'Firefly'
AUG	flowering ✳	C. v. 'Johnson's Variety'
SEPT	flowering ✳	C. v. 'Mair's Variety'
OCT	foliage 🌿	C. v. 'Peter Sparkes'
NOV	foliage 🌿	C. v. 'Wickwar Flame'
DEC	foliage 🌿	

CONDITIONS

Aspect Full bright sun is vital. The sun also emphasizes the colour of the foliage, its chief virtue in the winter garden.

Site These plants will only flourish in acid soil that is free draining. It should also be rich in well-rotted organic matter.

GROWING METHOD

Propagation Increase your number of plants by taking semi-ripe cuttings in the first part of summer. They root quickly.

Feeding Make sure that the soil has plenty of organic matter added to keep it rich and fertile.

Problems Only in extremely persistent humid conditions might heathers develop grey mould or disease. Otherwise, once planted, these are remarkably problem free.

FLOWERING

Season The flowers appear after midsummer, and continue their display right through into the autumn. There is a wide range of colours with dark red 'Allegro', white 'Beoley Gold', mauve 'Blazeaway', pink 'Elsie Purnell', and purple-pink 'Johnson's Variety'. The white 'Mair's Variety' makes good cut flowers.

PRUNING

General Give the plants a light prune in the spring if required, or for shape. Other than these cases, pruning is not necessary.

CAMPANULA
Bellflower

AS THE STARRY mauve-blue flowers appear, the bellflower plant seem to expand. It is a pretty plant that never fails to delight.

SCRAMBLING ALONG on its own or among other plants, the bellflower is undemanding and gives the gardener great rewards.

FEATURES

Partial Shade

Bellflowers are a large group of 300 species, varying from mat-like or rosette-forming plants to tall, upright species. These evergreen, groundcovering species are generally easy to grow, vigorous without being troublesome, good weed suppressors and delightful in flower. Flowers, appearing from midsummer, are mostly mauve-blue, although white forms are available. Plants are low growing, rarely exceeding 15cm (6in) in height but they can spread a good distance. Bellflowers can be grown as groundcover, in walls or in pots and troughs. They sometimes self-seed, appearing in cracks in paths or walls.

CAMPANULA AT A GLANCE

Campanula portenschlagiana is a moderate spreading bellflower with distinctive purple flowers in the summer. Hardy to −15°C (5°F).

JAN	foliage	RECOMMENDED VARIETIES	
FEB	foliage	*Campanula* 'Birch Hybrid'	
MAR	foliage	*C. cochleariifolia*	
APRIL	foliage	*C. garganica*	
MAY	foliage	*C. glomerata*	
JUNE	foliage	*C. poscharskyana*	
JULY	flowering	*C. pulla*	
AUG	flowering	*C. takesimana*	
SEPT	foliage	*C. portenschlagiana*	
OCT	foliage		
NOV	foliage		
DEC	foliage		

CONDITIONS

Aspect   Grows best in semi-shade or morning sun with afternoon shade.

Site   Soil must be well drained. *Campanula portenschlagiana* comes from the mountainous parts of Croatia. It is tolerant of a range of soil types but grows best in soil enriched with organic matter.

GROWING METHOD

Propagation   Increase stock by dividing clumps of rooted stems. The minute seed will also self-seed.

Feeding   Can be grown without supplementary fertilizer, but benefits from an application of complete plant food as growth commences in spring.

Problems   No specific problems are known.

FLOWERING

Season   Flowers profusely from mid-spring through to early summer. The flowers are a gorgeous rich purple, nearly 2.5cm (1in) long.

Cutting   Attractive though they are, the flowers are not suitable for cut-flower arrangements.

PRUNING

General   Remove spent flower stems. Once blooms have finished the entire flowering stem is easily and lightly pulled off.

CERASTIUM TOMENTOSUM
Snow-in-summer

THE FLOWER STEMS of snow-in-summer rise high above the silvery foliage. This plant likes dry conditions and flourishes on a steep slope.

FROM A DISTANCE this flowering mass truly looks like snow as it carpets the ground beneath a weeping mulberry.

FEATURES

Full Sun

Cerastium tomentosum is an attractive plant with small, silver-grey leaves and sprays of white flowers that appear in late spring and summer. The silvery foliage provides a good colour contrast with brighter colours in the garden. It has a low, creeping habit with stems that root down as they travel along. Ideal for sunny rockeries and dry areas, it is quite quick growing and long lived in the right conditions. Position the plants at about 30cm (1ft) intervals for quick cover. Once it is established, *C. tomentosum* suppresses weeds well but it may also invade areas where it is not wanted. It is, however, a simple matter to dig out any offending sections.

CERASTIUM AT A GLANCE

Cerastium tomentosum is a vigorous, sun-loving, white-flowering spreader, excellent on any spare piece of ground. Hardy to −15°C (5°F).

		COMPANION PLANTS
JAN	/	Berberis
FEB	/	Cotoneaster
MAR	flowering ❀	Elaeagnus
APRIL	flowering ❀	Ilex
MAY	flowering ❀	Prunus
JUNE	flowering ❀	Pyracantha
JULY	foliage ✿	Rosa
AUG	foliage ✿	Viburnum
SEPT	foliage ✿	
OCT	/	
NOV	/	
DEC	/	

CONDITIONS

Aspect   This plant must be grown in full sun to achieve its potential.

Site   Soil must be well drained.

GROWING METHOD

Propagation   The easiest method of propagation is by division of a rooted clump, but tip cuttings may be taken in late spring and summer. Given the rate at which it spreads, it is unlikely you will need more plants.

Feeding   Apply complete plant food or pelleted poultry manure in early spring. However, feeding is unnecessary, and snow-in-summer is almost as vigorous on quite poor soil.

Problems   This plant has no specific pest or disease problems, but overwatering or poorly drained soil will cause plants to rot and die.

FLOWERING

Season   Pretty white flowers are produced through spring and into early summer in cool areas.

PRUNING

General   No pruning is needed beyond shearing off spent flower stems or trimming growth to control its spread. You can be as ruthless as you want. *C. tomentosum* is quite tough, and keeps coming back even when you thought you'd pruned it excessively hard.

COTONEASTER
Horizontal Cotoneaster

PINK AND WHITE FLOWERS stud the stiff branches of this horizontal cotoneaster. It requires very little care.

THE BRILLIANT DISPLAY of red cotoneaster berries gives pleasure over many weeks. Here it grows with a small cyclamen.

FEATURES

Full Sun

Cotoneaster horizontalis is a deciduous spreading plant, ideal for banks and walls where the slightly arching stems can be seen to advantage. It will spread 1.5m (5ft) wide but rarely more than 1m (3ft) high. The horizontal stems are covered in small, dark green, shiny leaves that may turn reddish before falling in winter. In late spring *C. horizontalis* has small flowers that are white and pink in colour, but the main decorative effect comes from the long-lasting display of small, red berries. They follow the flowers in autumn and will persist on the plant into winter.

COTONEASTER A GLANCE

Cotoneaster horizontalis is a superb spreading shrub, with good shape and a long season of bright red berries. Hardy to −18°C (0°F).

		RECOMMENDED VARIETIES
JAN	/	*Cotoneaster adpressus*
FEB	/	*C. atropurpureum*
MAR	/	*C. cashmeriensis*
APRIL	/	*C.* 'Herbstfeuer'
MAY	flowering ✽	*C. horizontalis*
JUNE	foliage	*C. nanshan*
JULY	foliage	*C. perpusillus*
AUG	foliage	*C. rotundifolius*
SEPT	foliage	*C. divaricatus* 'Valkenburg'
OCT	foliage	
NOV	/	
DEC	/	

CONDITIONS

Aspect
Prefers full sun. The evergreen kind are the best choice for shadier positions. Position where it can be well seen in winter, ideally with the sun striking the berries. They really light up the scene.

Site
Cotoneasters tolerate a very wide range of soils but they are at their best in soils enriched with organic matter.

GROWING METHOD

Propagation
Can be grown from ripe seed removed from the fleshy berries and also from semi-hardwood cuttings taken in autumn.

Feeding
Apply complete plant food in early spring as growth commences.

Problems
No specific problems are known.

FLOWERING

Season
The small white and pink flowers appear from middle to late spring.

Berries
The berries colour up during early autumn and may persist until midwinter.

PRUNING

General
Pruning is not necessary unless it is to train the plant. It is traditionally grown against a fence or wall with branches spread along it.

DIANTHUS DELTOIDES
Maiden pink

A PROLIFIC SHOW of flowers can always be expected from this pretty dianthus, one of the many known as pinks.

SPILLING OVER a gravel path, this pink dianthus revels in the full sun and sharp drainage afforded by the small stones.

FEATURES

Full Sun

There are about 300 species of dianthus, including annual and perennial growers, and several of the alpine dianthus make low mounded growth suitable for groundcover. This species, *Dianthus deltoides*, makes a delightful groundcover with its thick, spreading mat-like growth. Foliage height rarely reaches more than 12cm (4³/₄in), while the pretty, fringed flowers stand about 20cm (8in) high. Flowers in the species, which appear in the summer, are deep rose pink but there are cultivars with flowers in various colours, including white, red and other shades of pink. In good conditions one plant can spread to 45cm (18in).

DIANTHUS AT A GLANCE

Dianthus deltoides is a low spreading perennial producing marvellous white, pink or red summer flowers. Hardy to −15°C (5°F).

JAN	foliage 🌱	RECOMMENDED VARIETIES
FEB	foliage 🌱	*Dianthus armeria*
MAR	foliage 🌱	'Doris'
APRIL	foliage 🌱	*D. erinaceus*
MAY	foliage 🌱	*D.* 'Haytor White'
JUNE	flowering ❀	*D.* 'Joe Vernon'
JULY	flowering ❀	*D.* 'Mrs Sinkins'
AUG	flowering ❀	*D. pavonius*
SEPT	foliage 🌱	*D. scardicus*
OCT	foliage 🌱	*D. superbus*
NOV	foliage 🌱	
DEC	foliage 🌱	

CONDITIONS

Aspect Prefers full sun all day. Keep away from anywhere remotely shady.

Site Soil must be well drained, and decayed organic matter added well ahead of planting time is beneficial. Very acid soils should be dressed with lime. Heavy clay soils need to be thoroughly broken up before planting with plenty of sand and horticultural grit.

GROWING METHOD

Propagation Grow from division of rooted sections of an existing plant, or from cuttings taken in late summer. Make sure that the cutting is a non-flowering one.

Feeding Give complete plant food in spring.

Problems No specific problems are known, but keep an eye out for aphids and slugs. Tackle the latter either with slug pellets or, if you don't want to use chemicals, instigate a nightly patrol, picking them off when seen.

FLOWERING

Season Flowers appear in the summer.

Cutting The flowers may be cut for posies but the stems are rather short.

PRUNING

General Shear off flowers once they have faded. No other pruning is needed.

ERICA CARNEA
Erica

A WHOLE SECTION of hillside is blanketed in colour. Flowering at the end of winter, ericas herald the coming of spring.

THE SMALL FLOWERS and dark green foliage of this erica create a frothy white mass. Ericas are at their best in full sunshine.

FEATURES

Full Sun

Otherwise known as winter or alpine heath, this is a small evergreen shrub growing about 25cm (10in) high at most, and spreading twice that distance. At its best on acid soil it will, however, tolerate some lime. The great virtue of ericas is that they provide indispensable winter foliage colour. *Erica carnea* has dark green leaves and dark pink flowers that last from winter well into early spring. Other excellent forms of erica include 'Adrienne Duncan' with bronze tinged foliage, 'Ann Sparkes' with lime green leaves, and 'Challenger' with rich red flowers. 'Golden Starlet' has white flowers and pale green foliage, and 'Vivellii' bronze leaves with pink flowers. The best way to grow ericas is in 'patchwork quilts', with great sheets of merging and contrasting colours.

ERICA AT A GLANCE

Erica carnea is a fine shrub with a wide range of excellent forms. A 'must' on acid soil. Hardy to −18°C (0°F).

		RECOMMENDED VARIETIES
JAN	flowering ❀	*Erica carnea*
FEB	flowering ❀	E. c. 'Adrienne Duncan'
MAR	flowering ❀	E. c. 'Ann Sparkes'
APRIL	flowering ❀	E. c. 'Challenger'
MAY	foliage 🍃	E. c. 'December Red'
JUNE	foliage 🍃	E. c. 'King George'
JULY	foliage 🍃	E. c. 'March Seedling'
AUG	foliage 🍃	E. c. 'Myretoun Ruby'
SEPT	foliage 🍃	E. c. 'Springwood White'
OCT	foliage 🍃	E. c. 'Vivellii'
NOV	foliage 🍃	
DEC	foliage 🍃	

CONDITIONS

Aspect Ericas need as much sun as they can get. They not only thrive in it, but you can really appreciate the full range of hues and tones. In darker parts of the garden their virtues will not stand out.

Site Moist, acid soil is the key. *Erica carnea* is unusual because it can tolerate slightly more alkaline conditions.

GROWING METHOD

Propagation The simplest method involves taking semi-ripe cuttings during the first part of summer.

Feeding This is not necessary. You can scatter ericaceous compost round new plants to give them a head start.

Problems They can suffer from fungal attacks in very humid conditions, but this is extremely unlikely. Otherwise, quite indestructible.

FLOWERING

Season *E. carnea* and its various excellent forms flower from around Christmas well into spring. There is a wide range of colours, many showing up well against the foliage which ranges from yellow lime green to bronze.

PRUNING

General This certainly is not necessary to keep plants in check since growth is very slow. You can prune to shape though, and this is best done after flowering in the spring before new growth appears.

GERANIUM
Cranesbill

THESE BLOOMS OF Geranium *'Johnson's Blue' appear in the summer, and contrast well with the light green foliage.*

THE ROUNDED FORMS of the G. *'Johnson's Blue' flowers are set off perfectly by the intricate shapes of this sun-loving plant's leaves.*

FEATURES

Sun or Part Shade

There is a terrific choice of excellent geraniums, and one that always makes it to the top of the list is 'Johnson's Blue'. It grows about 40cm (16in) high and double that in width. Right through the summer it is covered in rich blue flowers. It can be grown in the border, under apple trees, and to cover a spare patch of ground. It is easy to get hooked and start collecting more. 'Ann Folkard' has magenta flowers, grows 60cm (2ft) high, and flops 1m (3ft) wide or more. And *G. psilostemon* stands up 1.2m (4ft) high, extends 60cm (2ft) wide, giving more rich, magenta flowers. Most geraniums are in the soft pink, lavender-blue, or white range. Easy to grow, they quickly make decent-sized perennials.

GERANIUM AT A GLANCE

Geranium 'Johnson's Blue' is one of the very best hardy geraniums, giving a long summer of rich blue flowers. Hardy to −15°C (5°F).

		RECOMMENDED VARIETIES
JAN	/	*Geranium* 'Ann Folkard'
FEB	/	G. *endressii*
MAR	/	G. *himalayense* 'Gravetye'
APRIL	/	G. 'Johnson's Blue'
MAY	foliage	G. x *oxonianum* 'Wargrave
JUNE	flowering	Pink'
JULY	flowering	G. *pratense* 'Mrs Kendall
AUG	flowering	Clark'
SEPT	foliage	G. *psilostemon*
OCT	foliage	G. *sylvaticum* 'Mayflower'
NOV	/	
DEC	/	

CONDITIONS

Aspect The more sun the better. Note that when deciding where to grow 'Johnson's Blue', the colour blue always appears much more intense in early evening as the light fades. That's the time of day when it really stands out.

Site Typical garden soil is fine, with average fertility and decent drainage. Avoid extreme conditions of wet and over-dry soil.

GROWING METHOD

Propagation The easiest way to give yourself more 'Johnson's Blue' is to take a spade and slice vertically through the plant in the spring. Make sure each section has a good root system. You can still do this in the autumn.

Feeding If the soil is on the poor side, bump up the fertility with a slow-release fertilizer in the spring. Or mulch around the plant with well-rotted organic matter.

Problems Geraniums tend to dislike having cold wet roots all through the winter. Some of the species need very good winter drainage. Add horticultural sand or grit to the soil to improve drainage if required.

FLOWERING

Season Right through the summer.

PRUNING

General This really is not necessary.

HEDERA HELIX
Common ivy

THE RICH GREEN LEAVES *of ivy can be trimmed and trained into a variety of shapes, including this striking circle.*

COMMON IVY *is used here to spill over a retaining wall. In such a situation it will need very little trimming.*

FEATURES

Sun, Shade or Part Shade

Hedera helix is generally thought of as a climbing plant but it can also make an excellent, low-maintenance groundcover, with a dense mass of foliage. It is especially good in shady areas under trees and will readily climb up them, but keep ivy away from ornamental trees or they will quickly be obscured. *H. helix* may also be used in place of a lawn in formal areas where it is kept well clipped, and it is also suitable for planting where it can spill over a wall or bank. The straight species has very dark green, lobed leaves, but there are many dozens of cultivars with leaves edged, spotted or streaked with cream or gold, as well as great variation in leaf shape and size.

HEDERA AT A GLANCE

Hedera helix is a first-rate evergreen climber that also can be used as groundcover, and to romp over sheds, etc. Hardy to −18°C (0°F).

JAN	foliage 🌿	RECOMMENDED VARIETIES
FEB	foliage 🌿	*Hedera helix*
MAR	foliage 🌿	*H. h.* 'Angularis Aurea'
APRIL	foliage 🌿	*H. h.* 'Atropurpurea'
MAY	foliage 🌿	*H. h.* 'Buttercup'
JUNE	foliage 🌿	*H. h.* 'Glacier'
JULY	foliage 🌿	*H. h.* 'Ivalace'
AUG	foliage 🌿	*H. h.* 'Pedita'
SEPT	foliage 🌿	*H. h.* 'Shamrock'
OCT	flowering ❀	*H. h.* 'Spetchley'
NOV	foliage 🌿	
DEC	foliage 🌿	

CONDITIONS

Aspect Tolerates full sun but is at its best in dappled sunlight or shade. A wonderfully adaptable plant for which a place can generally be found in the garden.

Site Grows in poor soil, but best in moisture-retentive soil enriched with organic matter.

GROWING METHOD

Propagation It is easy to strike from semi-ripe tip cuttings taken through summer and early autumn. It roots easily from layers, too. You can even take spring cuttings and stick them straight back in the soil.

Feeding Apply complete plant food in early spring.Unless the soil is in a very poor state though, ivy can be left to get on with it.

Problems No special problems are known.

FLOWERING

Season Tiny, inconspicuous flowers are produced only on very mature, adult foliage and are never seen on plants that are kept clipped.

Berries Blue-black berries follow the flowers.

PRUNING

General Restrict pruning to cutting off wayward stems or keeping the plant within bounds. Trim in any season, but severe cutting is best in late winter, just before new growth.

HOSTA 'FRANCEE'
Plantain lily

THIS FINE SPECIMEN of a Hosta 'Francee' demonstrates how the plant forms dense mounds of foliage. An excellent groundcover plant.

THE MAIN ATTRACTION of the hostas in general are their variegated foliage, especially this H. 'Francee' with its white edges.

FEATURES

Sun, Shade or Part Shade

Every garden has room for a hosta. They are grown for their marvellous, decorative foliage which provides shade for the frogs and keeps down the weeds. 'Francee' stands out with its white margined leaves. Grow it with different coloured hostas like the bluish-leaved 'Hadspen Blue', which makes a neat, dense clump. 'Frances Williams' is blue-green with a yellowish margin. And 'Patriot' is another excellent white-edged hosta if you cannot get hold of 'Francee'. They can also be mass planted near water features, or just allowed to multiply in the shade under trees. With room for one only, try growing it in a pot, topping the soil with pebbles to set it off.

HOSTA AT A GLANCE

Hosta 'Francee' is a vigorous, clump-forming perennial that provides marvellous groundcover. Hardy to −18°C (0°F).

		RECOMMENDED VARIETIES
JAN	/	*Hosta* 'Aureomarginata'
FEB	/	H. 'Blue Angel'
MAR	/	H. 'Francee'
APRIL	foliage	H. 'Frances Williams'
MAY	foliage	H. 'Golden Tiara'
JUNE	foliage	H. 'Love Pat'
JULY	flowering	H. 'Patriot'
AUG	foliage	H. 'Shade Fanfare'
SEPT	foliage	H. 'Wide Brim'
OCT	foliage	
NOV	/	
DEC	/	

CONDITIONS

Aspect Most hostas grow in full sun if well watered. They also thrive in shade or dappled light. The blue-leaved kind are the hardest to place because they turn green with too much or too little shade. The yellow forms are best with direct sun either early or late in the day.

Site Provide rich, moisture-retentive soil. Add well-decayed manure to the ground before planting, and mulch afterwards. Avoid dry, free-draining, infertile ground.

GROWING METHOD

Propagation Divide the fleshy rhizomes in early spring. Most hostas perform best if they are divided every four to five years.

Feeding Apply scatterings of pelleted poultry manure in the spring.

Problems The chief enemies of these plants are slugs and snails which can devastate the incredibly attractive foliage. Spread sharp sand around the plants to deter intruders and use traps or bait.

FLOWERING

Season The white or pale violet flower spikes are interesting and usually appear in the summer, but the chief attraction has to be the foliage.

PRUNING

General Not necessary

HOUTTUYNIA CORDATA
Houttuynia

THIS WELL-ESTABLISHED Houttuynia cordata *is flourishing in a moist soil, although it would also provide good cover in a dry site.*

DECORATIVE VARIEGATED LEAVES splashed with cream and brilliant red are the most striking feature of the cultivar 'Chameleon'.

FEATURES

Shade

This is a groundcover plant for marshy, damp, cool parts of the garden, and can even grow in shallow water. In the right conditions the species makes a decent spreader, and can in fact become quite invasive. Its two most distinguishing features are that it has marvellously scented leaves, with the aroma of citrus fruit, and these turn reddish in the autumn. There are two good forms, slightly less invasive than the species, 'Chameleon' and 'Flore Pleno'. The first has fantastically eyecatching foliage. It has four colours, bronze, red, yellow, and dark green. The second, which is much harder to find, has white cones of petals. A highly useful plant.

HOUTTUYNIA AT A GLANCE

Houttuynia cordata is an excellent stream-side plant that spreads well and provides fresh white spring flowers.

		COMPANION PLANTS
JAN	/	
FEB	/	Camassia
MAR	/	Euphorbia
APRIL	foliage 🍂	Francoa
MAY	flowering ❀	Gentiana
JUNE	foliage 🍂	Gunnera
JULY	foliage 🍂	Heuchera
AUG	foliage 🍂	Hosta
SEPT	foliage 🍂	Iris
OCT	foliage 🍂	Ligularia
NOV	foliage 🍂	Lychnis
DEC	/	

CONDITIONS

Aspect Houttuynia grows in both full sun and light shade. 'Chameleon' gets better coloured leaves in the sun, where its colours look much more marked. Do not waste it in the shade.

Site The soil needs to be on the damp side, and rich with plenty of well-rotted organic matter.

GROWING METHOD

Propagation It is unlikely that you will ever need to propagate *H. cordata*, given how well it spreads, but you can easily make extra plants. Divide the plant in the spring, or take cuttings at the same time of year. The new growth quickly takes.

Feeding It is unlikely to need extra nutrients if grown in the right conditions.

Problems Apart from being attacked by slugs and snails, the only problem you might encounter is when trying to grow it in a basket in the water. It will need regular potting up to stop it bursting out of the container.

FLOWERING

Season The flowers appear in the spring, and show up well against the foliage.

PRUNING

General This is rarely necessary. Use a spade to slice off any unwanted, excess spread.

JUNIPERUS CONFERTA
Shore juniper

SOFT LOOKING but prickly to the touch, these mature juniper branches display pretty, blue-green berries, rarely seen on this species.

AN EXUBERANT PLANTING of juniper here cascades down a wall. A large expanse of this plant can be very striking.

FEATURES

Full Sun

This plant is known as shore juniper because it originates from coastal regions of Japan. It has soft, green, needle-like foliage which is very dense and prickly to the touch. Spreading with horizontal branches, juniper is an excellent groundcover for large areas as it may ultimately have a spread of 2.4m (8ft). It can, of course, be grown on flat ground but it also looks attractive on banks or spilling over walls. It is fairly fast growing for a conifer – it may spread 60cm (2ft) in a year in ideal conditions – and is long lived. There are also a number of other horizontal junipers worth considering. For example, *J. horizontalis* and its many cultivars have a range of leaf colours and forms. 'Wiltonii' is one of the best.

JUNIPERUS AT A GLANCE

Juniperus conferta is a reliable, fast-spreading evergreen conifer that can be snipped into attractive shapes. Hardy to –18°C (0°F).

JAN	foliage 🌣	RECOMMENDED VARIETIES
FEB	foliage 🌣	*Juniperus chinensis* 'Kaizuka'
MAR	foliage 🌣	*J. communis* 'Prostrata'
APRIL	foliage 🌣	*J. conferta*
MAY	foliage 🌣	*J. c.* 'Blue Pacific'
JUNE	foliage 🌣	*J. horizontalis*
JULY	foliage 🌣	*J. sabina tamariscifolia*
AUG	foliage 🌣	*J. squamata* 'Blue Star'
SEPT	foliage 🌣	*J. virginiana* 'Grey Owl'
OCT	foliage 🌣	
NOV	foliage 🌣	
DEC	foliage 🌣	

CONDITIONS

Aspect
This juniper grows best in full sun. It is tolerant of exposed windy sites and even full coastal exposure. Like *Cotoneaster horizontalis* it is a good plant by the water's edge, providing shade for fish and a place for frogs to hide.

Site
Soil must be well drained. The addition of decayed organic matter to the soil well ahead of planting should ensure good establishment and growth.

GROWING METHOD

Propagation
Grow from tip cuttings taken in the summer, or from short 5–7.5cm (2–3 in) long lateral growths taken with a heel of older wood during the same period

Feeding
Apply complete plant food or pelleted poultry manure in early spring.

Problems
No specific problems are known.

FLOWERING

Products
Juniper is a conifer, not a flowering plant.

PRUNING

General
Little or no pruning is needed unless it is necessary to control a wayward upright shoot. However, it is worth stressing that it can become quite a large, wayward and blobby plant if left untouched. Prune to shape, creating spaces for bulbs, and even for annual climbers to spread across it.

LAMIUM
Dead nettle

SOFT PINK FLOWERS and foliage boldly striped in silver make dead nettle a very desirable groundcover for any garden.

THE FOLIAGE of this dead nettle is almost entirely silver. It reflects any available light and will certainly give a lift to a shady corner.

FEATURES

Shade or
Part Shade

Despite its rather unattractive common name, *Lamium* is quite a pretty, soft-leaved groundcover that spreads by running stems (stolons) which root down as they spread. Some are very vigorous and may be invasive, and although individual plants are generally only 15–45cm (6–18 in) high, they can spread to cover 2m (6 ft) in warm, humid climates. There are many variegated forms with leaves splashed, speckled or spotted with silver or cream. Different species or cultivars produce flowers that may be pink, purple, cream or yellow. Dead nettle also makes a good basket plant. In the garden it is easy to grow and maintain, and is long lived.

LAMIUM AT A GLANCE

Lamium is a useful groundcover with small pretty leaves, but can be highly invasive. Hardy to −18°C (0°F).

		RECOMMENDED VARIETIES
JAN	/	*Lamium galeobdolon*
FEB	/	*L. galeobdolon* 'Hermann's
MAR	/	Pride'
APRIL	/	*L. garganicum*
MAY	foliage 🍃	*L. garganicum* 'Golden
JUNE	flowering ✳	Carpet'
JULY	flowering ✳	*L. maculatum*
AUG	flowering ✳	*L. m.* 'Aureum'
SEPT	foliage 🍃	*L. m.* 'Beacon Silver'
OCT	foliage 🍃	*L. m.* 'Cannon's Gold'
NOV	/	*L. m.* 'White Nancy'
DEC	/	

CONDITIONS

Aspect   *Lamium* does best in shade or semi-shade and when sheltered from strong wind.

Site   Tolerates a wide range of soils but is best in well-drained soils rich in organic matter. The ground should also be fairly moist.

GROWING METHOD

Propagation   Easily grown by dividing rooted plants. Alternatively you can grow from seed sown in the spring or autumn.

Feeding   Fertilizing is not necessary unless the soil is extremely poor, in which case complete plant food can be applied in early spring. An annual mulch with well-rotted organic matter also helps in this case.

Problems   There are no known problems.

FLOWERING

Season   Flowering spikes appear in the summer months, depending on species.

PRUNING

General   Pruning of plants is unnecessary but if they become too vigorous you may need to remove whole sections with a spade. If growing *L. galeobdolon*, you may need to insert a barrier into the soil to confine it. Use several thicknesses of builders' waterproofing plastic or metal sheeting, up to 30cm (1ft) deep.

LITHODORA DIFFUSA
Lithospermum

INTENSE ROYAL BLUE FLOWERS are the highlight of this lithospermum planting, which trails over a low retaining wall. The colour is intensified by the contrast with the chalk-white sweet Alice growing beside it.

FEATURES

Full Sun

This small, prostrate groundcover shrub is highly popular because of its brilliant blue flowers which cover the plant in late spring and early summer. It looks well and flourishes if grown in rockeries or on the edges of raised beds where it has perfect drainage. *Lithodora diffusa* can also be grown as a wall plant or between pavers or stepping stones. It does, however, need to be mass planted to get the best effect. There are a couple of cultivars available that have flowers either slightly larger than those of the species or in a different shade of blue, but it is, in fact, hard to beat the straight species for attractiveness.

LITHODORA AT A GLANCE

Lithodora diffusa is a shortish evergreen, 15cm (6in) high, with good forms making fine cover in acid soil. Hardy to −18°C (0°F).

JAN	foliage ❀	COMPANION PLANTS
FEB	foliage ❀	Azalea
MAR	foliage ❀	Calluna
APRIL	foliage ❀	Erica
MAY	flowering ❀	Gaultheria
JUNE	flowering ❀	Hydrangea
JULY	foliage ❀	Kalmia
AUG	foliage ❀	Pieris
SEPT	foliage ❀	Vaccinum
OCT	foliage ❀	
NOV	foliage ❀	
DEC	foliage ❀	

CONDITIONS

Aspect Needs full sun exposure. Do not attempt to hide it away in the shade. The consequent damp soil will also be a major problem.

Site This plant needs an acid soil. If you do not have acid soil in the garden it can be grown in tubs surrounding a feature plant.

GROWING METHOD

Propagation Grows from cuttings taken in late summer or from seed sown in autumn.

Feeding Apply complete plant food in spring as new growth commences.

Problems No pest or disease problems are known, but permanently wet and poorly drained soil will kill these plants.

FLOWERING

Season This evergreen shrub has a decent flowering period from late spring to early summer. To make sure that it is well seen, also try growing it on rockeries where it thrives with the excellent drainage. The forms 'Grace Ward' and 'Heavenly Blue' are the best and easiest to get.

Cutting Flowers are unsuitable for cutting.

PRUNING

General Lightly prune these plants after flowering to remove spent stems.

LYSIMACHIA NUMMULARIA
Creeping Jenny

THE SPECIES of creeping Jenny produces pretty yellow flowers and deep green foliage. Flowers are rarely seen on the golden form.

'AUREA', the golden cultivar of creeping Jenny, can be truly eye-catching when the sun strikes the yellow leaves.

FEATURES

Sun or
Part Shade

Usually seen in its golden-leaved form, 'Aurea', this groundcover has small, rounded leaves on stems that spread and root down as they go. The bright yellow leaves seem to light up the area where it is growing and it is often grown as a basket plant. Small, bright yellow flowers are produced in good conditions, and are more common on the plain species. Growth is flat, rarely more than 5cm (2in) above the ground and one plant will cover 50cm (20in) or so within a growing season, if conditions are good. *Lysimachia nummularia* can be long lived.

CONDITIONS

Aspect   Grow *L. nummularia* in either sun or semi-shade but always give it some protection from

LYSIMACHIA AT A GLANCE

L. nummularia is a reliable ground-hugging spreader with a spread of small yellow flowers in summer. Hardy to −18°C (0°F).

		RECOMMENDED VARIETIES
JAN	/	*Lysimachia atropurpurea*
FEB	/	*L. ciliata*
MAR	/	*L. clethroides*
APRIL	/	*L. minoricensis*
MAY	foliage ❀	*L. nummularia* 'Aurea'
JUNE	flowering ❀	*L. thyrsiflora*
JULY	flowering ❀	*L. vulgaris*
AUG	foliage ❀	
SEPT	foliage ❀	
OCT	foliage ❀	
NOV	/	
DEC	/	

the hottest summer sun. The golden form will lose its bright colour unless it gets enough sun or bright light.

Site   Prefers a well-drained but moist soil rich in organic matter. It is well worth forking in plenty of compost before planting so that it gets off to an excellent start.

GROWING METHOD

Propagation   This plant is easily grown from division of the rooted sections of the parent plant. However, it also grows well from firm-tip cuttings that are taken during the summer months. They quickly start to root.

Feeding   Complete plant food may be applied in early spring, but unless soil is very poor this will not be necessary.

Problems   No specific problems are known but these plants will die if they are short of water during the summer months. If one group of plants is going to get watered during a drought, make sure *L. nummularia* is included.

FLOWERING

Season   Small, yellow flowers are produced right through the summer.

PRUNING

General   No general pruning is necessary but *L. nummularia* may need occasional trimming to confine its growth to the desired area. If the central growth starts to become thin, cut back some of the trailing stems to promote more growth from the centre.

NEPETA X FAASSENII
Catmint

THE SPIKES of mauve-blue catmint flowers persist over a long period and the bush, when grown in full sun, becomes quite dense.

WILD CATMINT or catnip, N. cataria, is the species most attractive to cats. Rubbing or bruising the foliage releases the unusual scent.

FEATURES

Sun or
Part Shade

The grey-green leaves of *Nepeta* x *faassenii* are a lovely foil for other, brighter colours in the garden. Its mauve-blue flowers are produced over a long period too, making this is a useful plant for a sunny spot in the garden. It is quite quick to establish and is fairly long lived. The height is rarely more than 30cm (1ft) and one plant may cover 45cm (18in) or so, making roots as it goes. The foliage is aromatic when bruised and can then be attractive to cats.
N. x *faassenii* is sometimes used as a cover planting between roses, especially old roses, as it provides a pleasing contrast in texture and colour. It is a great favourite for garden edgings and cottage garden plantings and can be grown in a hanging basket or container. There is a cultivar known as 'Six Hills Giant', which has taller growth and larger flowers.

NEPETA AT A GLANCE

N. x *faassenii* is an excellent plant for cottage gardens, with sprays of lavender flowers and greyish leaves. Hardy to −15°C (5°F).

		RECOMMENDED VARIETIES
JAN	/	*Nepeta* x *faassenii*
FEB	/	N. *govaniana*
MAR	/	N. *grandiflora*
APRIL	/	N. *nervosa*
MAY	foliage	N. *racemosa*
JUNE	flowering	N. 'Six Hills Giant'
JULY	flowering	
AUG	flowering	
SEPT	flowering	
OCT	foliage	
NOV	/	
DEC	/	

CONDITIONS

Aspect This plant grows best in full sun but tolerates shade for part of the day.

Site Needs well-drained soil and tolerates poor soils, but growth is best if some organic matter is dug in well ahead of planting time.

GROWING METHOD

Propagation *N.* x *faassenii* is easy to grow from rooted suckers, which are produced freely. It may also be grown from cuttings taken through summer. Alternatively, lift and divide established plants in the spring as active growth begins.

Feeding Does not generally need fertilizer, but if the soil is very poor, complete plant food may be applied in early spring. In good conditions extra feeding is not necessary.

Problems No specific problems are known but overwatering or heavy, poorly drained soil can eventually kill this plant.

FLOWERING

Season *N.* x *faassenii* has a long flowering period from early summer into early autumn. The colours are generally on the soft side being pale blue or lilac-pink. The best display is in early summer, but by cutting it back you promote fresh new growth and another good display.

PRUNING

General Cut back old growth in spring to promote young, fresh growth.

PACHYSANDRA TERMINALIS
Pachysandra

A LOVELY SHEEN is a feature of the foliage on this variegated form of pachysandra, while the cream leaf margins brighten the leaves and add interest to what is already a handsome plant. This is a long-term planting and is an ideal groundcover under trees.

FEATURES

Shade or Part Shade

Sometimes also known as Japanese spurge, this is an ideal groundcover under trees as it is happy in shade and tolerates dry soil. It has glossy, toothed leaves in a rosette form. Quite fast growing but long lived, it rarely grows more than 20cm (8in) high. It spreads with runners and makes a dense, weed-suppressing cover once established. Plant at about 30cm (1ft) intervals for quick cover. *Pachysandra terminalis* produces greenish white flower spikes in spring. There is a cultivar with white variegated leaves known as 'Variegata'.

PACHYSANDRA AT A GLANCE

Pachysandra terminalis is an evergreen with shiny dark leaves. White flowers appear in early summer . Hardy to −18°C (0°F).

		COMPANION PLANTS
JAN	foliage	
FEB	foliage	Euonymus
MAR	foliage	Hydrangea
APRIL	foliage	Mahonia
MAY	foliage	Phillyrea
JUNE	flowering ❀	Rubus
JULY	foliage	Sambucus
AUG	foliage	Skimmia
SEPT	foliage	Vaccinium
OCT	foliage	Viburnum
NOV	foliage	
DEC	foliage	

CONDITIONS

Aspect   Although tolerant of sun or shade, this plant is best in shaded and fairly sheltered positions.

Site   Tolerates damp or dry soil but not heavy, waterlogged clays.

GROWING METHOD

Propagation   Grows from divisions of older clumps lifted in the spring. Make sure that each section looks healthy, and has buds and roots, before replanting it in the garden.

Feeding   Apply complete plant food in early spring.

Problems   No specific problems are known.

FLOWERING

Season   Greenish white flower spikes are produced in the first part of summer but they are not very showy. Note that there are two other forms but that they do not offer a choice of flowers. 'Green Carpet' has finer, smaller leaves, and 'Variegata' has foliage with a white edge.

PRUNING

General   Pruning is not necessary. If growth becomes too dense and congested, it is a simple matter to thin it out – pull up unwanted plants, or lift clumps and replant the younger growths.

PERSICARIA AFFINIS
Persicaria

A STUNNING PLANTING of Persicaria affinis *makes a thick evergreen cover, enlivened by the long-lasting show of flowers.*

DENSE PINK SPIKES appear from midsummer, later highlighted against striking red-bronze autumn leaves.

FEATURES

Full Sun

Persicaria affinis is a very useful evergreen groundcover plant. It forms an extensive carpet of dark green foliage that turns brown-bronze in the autumn. The eyecatching 8cm (3in) long spikes of bright red flowers are held on stems well clear of the foliage. Individual plants grow about 30cm (1ft) high, and twice as wide. There are several excellent forms which many consider superior to the species. 'Darjeeling Red' has larger, 10cm (4in) long leaves, some even bigger, and two-tone flowers that start pink and darken to red. 'Donald Lowndes' has more pointy leaves, and pale then dark pink flowers. 'Superba' is pink tinged red, with bronze leaves in autumn.

PERSICARIA AT A GLANCE

Persicaria affinis is a remarkably reliable evergreen groundcover plant, with a long flowering season. Hardy to −15°C (5°F).

		COMPANION PLANTS
JAN	foliage	
FEB	foliage	Francoa
MAR	foliage	Geum
APRIL	foliage	Gunnera
MAY	foliage	Hellebore
JUNE	foliage	Hosta
JULY	flowering	Iris
AUG	flowering	Lychnis
SEPT	flowering	Primula
OCT	flowering	Rheum
NOV	foliage	
DEC	foliage	

CONDITIONS

Aspect It needs either bright sun or light shade. It should perform equally well in both.

Site Provided the soil is on the moist side and does not dry out, which is the key requirement, it should thrive. An excellent plant for growing near streams where the soil remains quite damp. In the right conditions it forms very good groundcover, and can even be invasive.

GROWING METHOD

Propagation The quickest method involves digging up plants in the spring or autumn, and dividing them into strong healthy sections. Make sure each has good roots.

Feeding This is rarely necessary.

Problems *P. affinis* and its forms are generally problem free, though slugs can attack fresh new growth. However, the forms which are most prone to slug and snail damage are *P. campanulata* and *P. virginiana*.

FLOWERING

Season Given plenty of sun, these plants should have a long flowering season. It begins about the middle of summer and graces the garden well into the autumn.

PRUNING

General Pruning is not necessary.

PHLOX SUBULATA
Alpine phlox

THE DAINTY FLOWERS *on alpine phlox create a tremendous impact when they are massed in full bloom.*

GROWN AS A BORDER *around beds of bulbs and perennials, this planting of alpine phlox is so full of flowers, the foliage is hidden.*

FEATURES

Full Sun

Phlox subulata grows about 15cm (6in) high and spreads into a mat about 50cm (20in) across. In bloom it is a mass of small, flattish flowers in white, pink, rose, mauve or blue. There are many named cultivars available and they can flower for several weeks. *P. subulata* grows ideally in rockeries, trailing over walls or on slightly sloping ground where excellent drainage is assured. Although plants last well over several years, the best blooming comes from younger plants. Start new plants every few years to maintain vigour.

PHLOX AT A GLANCE

Phlox subulata makes an evergreen mat of fresh green leaves with bright late spring flowers. Hardy to –15°C (5°F).

		RECOMMENDED VARIETIES
JAN	foliage	*Phlox adsurgens*
FEB	foliage	
MAR	foliage	*P. a.* 'Chattahoochee'
APRIL	foliage	*P. a.* 'Emerald Cushion'
MAY	flowering	*P. a.* 'Kelly's Eye'
JUNE	flowering	*P.* x *procumbens*
JULY	foliage	*P. subulata*
AUG	foliage	*P. s.* 'Amazing Grace'
SEPT	foliage	*P. s.* 'G. F. Wilson'
OCT	foliage	*P. s.* 'Marjorie'
NOV	foliage	*P. s.* 'McDaniel's Cushion'
DEC	foliage	*P. s.* 'Scarlet Flame'

CONDITIONS

Aspect   Grow this plant in full sun.
Site   Must have very well-drained soil (if it is at all on the heavy side, make sure that it is well broken up with plenty of horticultural sand and grit), but the soil need not be very rich.

GROWING METHOD

Propagation   Detach rooted sections from the parent plant in early spring, or take tip cuttings during summer and early autumn.
Feeding   Apply complete plant food as new growth begins in the spring.
Problems   No specific problems are known but poor drainage will rot the plants.

FLOWERING

Season   Flowers should be produced from mid-spring to early summer. For a colour contrast also grow 'Amazing Grace' which has pale pink flowers, 'Scarlet Flame' in scarlet, and 'Temiskaming' in magenta.
Cutting   Flowers are not suitable for cutting.

PRUNING

General   No pruning is needed beyond shearing off the spent flower heads.

PULMONARIA
Lungwort

A SHADY GARDEN AREA is enlivened by the mass of dark blue flowers that decorate Pulmonaria 'Lewis Palmer' during spring.

THE FUNNEL-SHAPED BLOOMS of Pulmonaria species are a prized feature, and some forms also have attractively variegated leaves.

FEATURES

Partial Shade

Pulmonaria is well suited to planting under trees, between shrubs or at the front of a shady border. The abundant flowers appear before the leaves have fully developed, and are mostly in shades of blue, pink, and white. The foliage is very handsome, often silver spotted, and if given a shearing after flowering produces a second, fresh mound of leaves. The whole plant rarely grows more than 25–30cm (10–12in) high, and when established is very decorative, even out of flower.

PULMONARIA AT A GLANCE

A genus of 14 species with deciduous and evergreen perennials. A flowering spreader for damp shade. Hardy to −18°C (0°F).

JAN	foliage ❀	RECOMMENDED VARIETIES
FEB	foliage ❀	*Pulmonaria angustifolia*
MAR	flowering ❀	*P. a.* 'Munstead Blue'
APRIL	flowering ❀	*P.* 'Lewis Palmer'
MAY	flowering ❀	*P. longifolia* 'Bertram
JUNE	foliage ❀	Anderson'
JULY	foliage ❀	*P. officinalis* Cambridge Blue
AUG	foliage ❀	Group
SEPT	foliage ❀	*P. officinalis* 'Sissinghurst
OCT	foliage ❀	White'
NOV	foliage ❀	*P. rubra*
DEC	foliage ❀	*P. saccharata* Argentea Group

CONDITIONS

Aspect Grows best in light shade, or in the borders that are shady during the hottest part of the day. The leaves quickly wilt under a hot sun.

Site The soil should be heavily enriched with decayed organic matter, but it also needs to drain quite well.

GROWING METHOD

Propagation Grows from ripe seed, or by division of clumps either after flowering or in the autumn. Replant divisions about 15cm (6in) apart. Better still, let plants freely hybridize. Young and established plants need moist soil during the growing season.

Feeding Apply a little complete fertilizer in early spring, and mulch well.

Problems No specific problems to worry about.

FLOWERING

Season *Pulmonaria* flowers in the spring.

Cutting The flowers last quite well in a vase.

PRUNING

General Only necessary when shearing over the plant to get a second flush of flowers.

ROSA HYBRIDS
Rose

'SNOW CARPET' is a lovely miniature rose that produces masses of flowers and very healthy foliage. It makes a beautiful groundcover.

THIS CARPET ROSE bears prolific bright pink flowers and looks spectacular when it is used as a groundcover.

FEATURES

Full Sun

Most people think of roses as shrubs, standards or climbers but there are a number of roses that can be used for groundcover. The 'Noatraum' rose, with its bright pink blooms, was introduced within the last few years and is deservedly popular for its long flowering period and disease resistance. There is also 'Snow Carpet', with masses of small white blooms, while the excellent Japanese 'Nozomi' has pink-white flowers. Look at rose catalogues for others that can be used this way.

CONDITIONS

Aspect   Must have full sun and good air circulation. and plenty of room to spread in all directions.

ROSA AT A GLANCE

Some roses make excellent flowering groundcover, adding an extra layer of interest. Hardy to −18°C (0°F).

		RECOMMENDED VARIETIES
JAN	/	*Rosa* 'Grouse'
FEB	/	R. 'Hertfordshire'
MAR	/	R. 'Magic Carpet'
APRIL	foliage 🌱	R. 'Max Graf'
MAY	foliage 🌱	R. 'Nozomi'
JUNE	flowering ❀	R. 'Raubritter'
JULY	flowering ❀	R. 'Snow Carpet'
AUG	foliage 🌱	R. 'Suffolk'
SEPT	foliage 🌱	
OCT	foliage 🌱	
NOV	/	
DEC	/	

Site   Soil should be well drained and well prepared by the addition of large amounts of organic matter. Add lime to acid soils.

GROWING METHOD

Propagation   Many of these roses strike fairly easily from cuttings of dormant wood taken in the autumn. Some roses must be budded on to species understocks.

Feeding   Apply complete plant food in spring and again in midsummer. Spreading an organic matter mulch round the plant in the spring will help to feed the soil.

Problems   Roses are vulnerable to attack by a number of garden pests and diseases. Aphids clustering on new growth can simply be hosed off or sprayed with pyrethrum. Black spot and powdery mildew can be troublesome in humid weather, you may have to resort to chemical spraying of the plants. Many groundcover roses have good resistance to these diseases.

FLOWERING

Season   A succession of blooms appear from summer to autumn, depending on the variety.

Cutting   Usually short stemmed, groundcover roses add to most cut flower displays.

PRUNING

General   Cut off spent flower stems throughout the season. The main rose pruning is done in early spring. At other times remove any dead, diseased or damaged wood.

ROSMARINUS OFFICINALIS

Rosemary

ROSEMARY IS typically seen as a herb but it also gives marvellous blue colour in the spring garden, when yellow tends to dominate.

THIS VERY HEALTHY prostrate rosemary is enjoying the sharp drainage provided by the raised garden bed.

FEATURES

Full Sun

The evergreen, prostrate-growing *Rosmarinus officinalis* 'Prostratus' has all the features of the shrubby rosemary, including highly aromatic, needle-like foliage and small-lobed blue flowers that appear among the leaves in spring. It looks lovely planted on top of a wall or raised garden bed where it can spill over, or it can be grown beside a path where it will be brushed by passers-by to release the strong fragrance. It is a very hardy plant and tolerant of a wide range of growing conditions. Rosemary is the herb of remembrance and fidelity and has many culinary and herbal uses.

ROSMARINUS AT A GLANCE

Rosemary can be trained into all kinds of shapes, but left alone, in time, makes a marvellous great scented bush. Hardy to –18°C (0°F).

		RECOMMENDED VARIETIES
JAN	foliage	*Rosmarinus officinalis*
FEB	foliage	*R. o.* var. *albiflorus*
MAR	flowering	*R. o.* 'Benenden Blue'
APRIL	flowering	*R. o.* 'Fota Blue'
MAY	flowering	*R. o.* 'Majorca Pink'
JUNE	flowering	*R. o.* 'Miss Jessopp's
JULY	foliage	Upright'
AUG	foliage	*R. o.* Prostratus Group
SEPT	foliage	*R. o.* 'Severn Sea'
OCT	foliage	*R. o.* 'Tuscan Blue'
NOV	foliage	
DEC	foliage	

CONDITIONS

Aspect Needs full sun and tolerates windy, exposed coastal conditions. Do not attempt to hide it away in the shade. Rosemary is naturally very slow growing so do not slow it down any more.

Site Soil must be well drained but this plant grows well in poor soils. Add lime or dolomite to very acid soils before planting.

GROWING METHOD

Propagation Grow from semi-ripe cuttings taken in the summer. If you need a quick effect it is worth buying well-established plants. However, if growing a rosemary hedge, one good-sized plant can yield hundreds of cuttings.

Feeding Little or no fertilizer is needed.

Problems No specific problems are known.

FLOWERING

Season The blue flowers are produced in spring. They generally last into early summer.

PRUNING

General Pruning is not necessary unless it is to trim a wayward upward branch or to train the plant to shape. However, by taking regular cuttings for cooking you will automatically keep pruning the plant.

SAPONARIA
Soapwort

THE STEMLESS PINK FLOWERS OF Saponaria 'Bressingham' seem to smother the foliage, making a strong and colourful impact.

DELICATE ROCK-GARDEN PLANTS are often grown singly, but S. 'Bressingham' is best densely planted as a filler or edging plant.

FEATURES

Full Sun

Saponaria includes plants for the border and wild garden, and for rock gardens. *S. officinalis* is the one for the former, making a brightly coloured invader – the form 'Rubra Plena' spreads more than most. *S.* 'Bressingham' provides good cover for a rock garden. It grows 8cm (3in) high, spreading 30cm (12in) wide, and has gorgeous, dark pink flowers. It is sometimes called 'Bressingham Hybrid'. The common name arises because the leaves of *S. officinalis* can be used as a kind of soap.

SAPONARIA AT A GLANCE

S. 'Bressingham' gives good perennial cover in the rock garden, producing eyecatching pink flowers in summer. Hardy to −15°C (5°F).

		RECOMMENDED VARIETIES
JAN	/	*Saponaria* 'Bressingham'
FEB	/	*S. caespitosa*
MAR	/	*S. ocymoides*
APRIL	/	*S. officinalis*
MAY	foliage 🍂	*S. o.* 'Alba Plena'
JUNE	flowering ✤	*S. o.* 'Rosea Plena'
JULY	flowering ✤	*S. o.* 'Rubra Plena'
AUG	foliage 🍂	*S.* x *olivana*
SEPT	foliage 🍂	
OCT	foliage 🍂	
NOV	/	
DEC	/	

CONDITIONS

Aspect This plant is exclusively for a place in full sun. Do not try to grow it anywhere else.

Site The soil needs to be reasonably fertile, but the main requirement is excellent drainage and plenty of added grit.

GROWING METHOD

Propagation You can either take cuttings in the first part of summer, or increase your stock and cover by sowing seed in the spring or the autumn. Note that each plant has a good spread though. You are unlikely to need many cuttings.

Feeding Do not attempt to over-feed, which is counter-productive. Average fertility is fine.

Problems The border plants can be shredded in extreme cases by slugs and snails, but because 'Bressingham' grows in the rockery, which contains gritty sharp stone in the soil, slugs will keep well away.

FLOWERING

Season A decent summer show of dark pink flowers.

PRUNING

General Not necessary.

SAXIFRAGA X URBIUM
London pride

SAXIFRAGA X URBIUM *is an easy plant to grow, and makes a graceful plant to flank a shady pathway through the garden.*

LEATHERY LEAVES WITH *unusual serrated edges contrast beautifully with the airy blooms that are held high above them.*

FEATURES

Full Shade

Saxifraga x *urbium* is a useful, quick-spreading, attractive plant producing scores of leathery, fresh green leaves. In summer whiteish-pink flowers appear on tall stems. It grows 30cm (1ft) high and is quite invasive. There are several other first-rate groundcover saxifrages. One is 'Bob Hawkins'. It forms a carpet of rosettes with variegated leaves, and white flowers tinged green in summer. It grows 20cm (8in) high, and spreads about 30cm (1ft). *S. exarata moschata* makes a cushion with cream or yellow star-like flowers. It is much shorter at 10cm (4in), and spreads about 30cm (1ft). The form 'Cloth of Gold' is even better and has gold coloured foliage that stands out.

SAXIFRAGA AT A GLANCE

Saxifraga x *urbium* is an extremely useful plant growing well in the shade. It is also a prodigious spreader. Hardy to −18°C (0°F).

JAN	foliage ✿	RECOMMENDED VARIETIES
FEB	foliage ✿	*Saxifraga* 'Bob Hawkins'
MAR	foliage ✿	*S. cuneifolia*
APRIL	foliage ✿	*S. exarata moschata*
MAY	foliage ✿	*S. marginata*
JUNE	flowering ❃	*S. paniculata*
JULY	flowering ❃	*S. sempervivum*
AUG	foliage ✿	*S.* x *urbium*
SEPT	foliage ✿	
OCT	foliage ✿	
NOV	foliage ✿	
DEC	foliage ✿	

CONDITIONS

Aspect *S.* x *urbium* thrives in the shade, both light and deep. Keep it out of the sun.

Site The best soil for *S.* x *urbium* is moist and rich, with plenty of well-rotted organic matter added before planting. An annual spring mulch around the base should boost its performance, with extra rosettes.

GROWING METHOD

Propagation *S.* x *urbium* can easily be increased by taking off a rosette in the spring, and treating it as a cutting. It will quickly root. You can also sow by seed in the autumn.

Feeding Given rich, moist soil, this plant should not need extra nutrients. It only requires a boost on poor soil.

Problems The biggest problem comes from slugs and snails. Both can devastate the young foliage. Use slug pellets as required, or keep a look out at night by torchlight.

FLOWERING

Season The flowers appear in the summer. They are held high above the foliage.

PRUNING

General The only pruning necessary is to slice off unwanted spreading growth to keep London pride in a particular area.

SOLEIROLIA SOLEIROLII
Baby's tears

THE TINY LEAVES of baby's tears grow very thickly, making it a good weed suppressor. It looks good even in shaded and moist conditions.

BABY'S TEARS will grow over any surface. Although considered a problem by some people, it will flourish where other plants struggle.

FEATURES

Shade or Part Shade

Although native to the western Mediterranean and Italy, this flat, mat-forming, creeping groundcover with tiny leaves flourishes in shady, damp conditions. It is known by many other common names, including mind-your-own-business, Irish moss, Japanese moss, Corsican curse and Corsican carpet plant. It is often used as a surface cover around the base of potted plants and as a groundcover under shrubs in shady areas. It can become rather weedy as it grows from seeds shed from its inconspicuous flowers, and from small pieces detached from the main growth. In its preferred damp, shady habitat, it is both long lived and persistent.

SOLEIROLIA AT A GLANCE

Soleirolia soleirolii is a fantastically invasive spreader with tiny white flowers in summer. Hardy to −15°C (5°F).

JAN	foliage	
FEB	foliage	RECOMMENDED VARIETIES
MAR	foliage	*Soleirolia soleirolii* 'Aurea'
APRIL	foliage	*S. s.* 'Variegata'
MAY	foliage	
JUNE	flowering	COMPANION PLANTS
JULY	flowering	Gunnera
AUG	foliage	Lysichiton
SEPT	foliage	Lysimachia
OCT	foliage	Primrose
NOV	foliage	
DEC	foliage	

CONDITIONS

Aspect   Grows best in shady, damp areas or where it receives dappled sunlight. So do not plant in direct sun as this may cause burning, especially during the height of summer.

Site   *Soleirolia soleirolii* will grow in a range of soil types but it prefers well-drained soils that are rich in organic matter. It makes good cover near a stream where the conditions are often ideal, but note that it is a rapid spreader. Check that it will not throttle nearby ornamental plants.

GROWING METHOD

Propagation   *S. soleirolii* will usually propagate itself, sometimes where it is not wanted, but new plants can be started easily from small sections of rooted stems.

Feeding   Fertilizing is not generally necessary.

Problems   No specific problems are known.

FLOWERING

Season   Flowers can be very tiny and very difficult to see fully without a magnifying glass.

PRUNING

General   As *S. soleirolii* is a flat-growing plant, pruning is not necessary. However, you may find that it is necessary to cut back sections of the mat if it becomes too invasive.

STACHYS BYZANTINA
Lamb's ears

THE LEAVES OF Stachys byzantina *have the texture of soft velvet, making them one of the most inviting plants in the garden.*

THESE INVALUABLE lush, green carpeters are commonly grown as edging in flower borders and rock gardens.

FEATURES

Full Sun

Stachys byzantina is a low-growing, evergreen perennial often used as an edging plant. It is good in rose beds, but wherever it is planted it must have excellent drainage and full sun. The leaves are densely covered with hairs, giving them a white or pale grey woolly appearance, hence its common name. It produces pink-purple flowers on spikes that stand above the foliage, but they are not especially attractive; it is usually grown for its foliage, and not the flowers. The exceptions are *Stachys macrantha* 'Robusta' and *S. officinalis*. 'Cotton Ball' has woolly flowers good for dried arrangements. Plants grow 15–20cm (6–8in) high, but spread a good distance.

STACHYS AT A GLANCE

Stachys byzantina is a superb, silver-leaved plant that always catches the eye. Well worth growing in every garden. Hardy to −18°C (0°F).

		RECOMMENDED VARIETIES
JAN	/	*Stachys byzantina*
FEB	/	*S. b.* 'Cotton Ball'
MAR	/	*S. b.* 'Primrose Heron'
APRIL	foliage	*S. coccinea*
MAY	foliage	*S. macrantha*
JUNE	flowering	*S. m.* 'Robusta'
JULY	flowering	*S. officinalis*
AUG	flowering	
SEPT	foliage	
OCT	foliage	
NOV	/	
DEC	/	

CONDITIONS

Aspect   Full sun is essential all day for the plants to thrive and perform well.

Site   Needs very fast-draining soil. It grows well in poor sandy or gravelly soil. Avoid thick, wet, heavy clay at all costs.

GROWING METHOD

Propagation   *S. byzantina* grows readily from cuttings that are taken in the spring or autumn. The new divisions must be planted out about 20cm (8in) apart. Water new plants regularly. Once they are established, they need to be watered very occasionally.

Feeding   Grows without supplementary fertilizer, but a little complete plant food can be applied in the early spring.

Problems   There are no specific problems but container plants will quickly fail if they are over-watered, and border plants will rot if they become waterlogged.

FLOWERING

Season   The flowers are produced in the summer, sometimes into autumn. But the tactile grey foliage is by far the chief attraction.

PRUNING

General   Pruning is rarely necessary. If any cutting back is needed do it in early spring.

SYMPHYTUM OFFICINALE
Comfrey

SYMPHYTUM CAUCASICUM *is a vigorous and tolerant plant that is often used as groundcover in wilder parts of the garden.*

THE BELL-SHAPED FLOWERS *of* Symphytum *are held in clusters above the foliage, and festoon the plant in spring and summer.*

FEATURES

Sun or
Part Shade

Symphytum officinale is one of the best groundcovering plants. In the right conditions, just one plant can spread 2m (6ft), even climbing over low walls. *S. officinale* has a mass of violet, pink or yellow flowers. Experts prefer other forms like *S.* x *uplandicum* 'Variegatum', which has superb grey-green leaves with a creamy-white edge. The flowers are lilac-pink. The only problem is that it can revert to a dark green leaf, especially in the wrong conditions. It is much less invasive than *S. officinale*, with one plant spreading 60cm (2ft). 'Goldsmith' also has attractive foliage, dark green leaves with cream markings around the outside, but spreads about half as much as 'Variegatum', which has leaves edged in white

SYMPHYTUM AT A GLANCE

Symphytum officinale is a reliable, free-spreading, spring-flowering perennial. The dark leaves are tough and hairy. Hardy to −18°C (0°F).

		RECOMMENDED VARIETIES
JAN	/	*Symphytum caucasicum*
FEB	/	S. 'Goldsmith'
MAR	/	S. 'Hidcote Blue'
APRIL	/	S. *ibericum*
MAY	flowering ❀	S. *officinale*
JUNE	flowering ❀	S. *tuberosum*
JULY	foliage 🍃	S. x *uplandicum* 'Variegatum'
AUG	foliage 🍃	
SEPT	foliage 🍃	
OCT	foliage 🍃	
NOV	foliage 🍃	
DEC	foliage 🍃	

CONDITIONS

Aspect   This plant thrives in either full sun or partial, dappled shade, such as woodland areas.

Site   The soil needs to be on the damp side and quite fertile. Clay soil that has been reasonably broken up and lightened is ideal. *S. officinale* should spread quite quickly.

GROWING METHOD

Propagation   With a fast spreader like *S. officinale*, there is no need to propagate. But when you need more plants to colonize another area, divide plants in the spring. They quickly settle. Close planting gives more immediate cover but just a few plants will give good cover over 2.4m (8ft) or so.

Feeding   Assuming that the plant is growing in clay soil which is perfectly fertile, additional feeding is not necessary. Otherwise, give a little slow-release fertilizer in spring.

Problems   *S. officinale* is a remarkably tough and resourceful plant, which is easy to grow and attracts very few problems.

FLOWERING

Season   The flowers appear in the spring and early summer. The species which produces the most distinctive coloured flowers is *S. caucasicum*, which has bright blue blooms .

Pruning   Only prune if it is necessary to confine the plant's growth. Slice off any unwanted growth with a spade. Otherwise, let the plant spread wherever it wants.

THYMUS
Thyme

WOOLLY THYME is a carpeting plant often grown in gaps between pavers and paths. The tiny leaves are covered in dense hairs.

A SMALL THYME LAWN here forms a neat green triangle. In this open, sunny spot it thrives and needs little maintenance.

FEATURES

Full Sun

There are over 300 species of thyme, many of which are suitable for use as groundcovers. *Thymus serpyllum*, which reaches 25cm (10in) in height, is commonly grown this way, as is *T. polytrichus* which grows 5cm (2in) high and 60cm (2ft) wide. These and others thymes have a creeping, mat-like habit, rooting down at the nodes as they grow. They are tough, low-maintenance groundcovers for hot, dry spots between paving stones, in rockeries or along the edges of garden or raised beds. All have aromatic foliage that releases its scent when bruised or crushed – you can step on them occasionally. The leaves can also be used in cooking. The small pink or mauve flowers are very attractive to bees.

THYMUS AT A GLANCE

Thymes give three plants in one. Good groundcover, pretty flowers, and excellent herbs for cooking. Hardy to –15°C (5°F).

JAN	foliage	
FEB	foliage	
MAR	foliage	
APRIL	foliage	
MAY	foliage	
JUNE	flowering	
JULY	flowering	
AUG	foliage	
SEPT	foliage	
OCT	foliage	
NOV	foliage	
DEC	foliage	

RECOMMENDED VARIETIES

Thymus x *citriodorus*
T. x *c.* 'Aureus'
T. x *c.* 'Bertram Anderson'
T. 'Coccineus'
T. 'Doone Valley'
T. herba-barona
T. serphyllum coccineus
T. vulgaris

CONDITIONS

Aspect Needs full sun all day. These are mainly Mediterranean plants used to long hot summers, with the minimum amount of shade.

Site Soil must be well drained but it need not be rich. Add lime to very acid soils before planting. Heavy wet ground needs to be thoroughly broken up, with large handfuls of horticultural sand and grit around the plant. If the roots stay cold and wet over winter, the plants will not survive.

GROWING METHOD

Propagation Firm-tip cuttings can be taken at any time through the spring and summer. Rooted sections of plants can be dug up and transplanted during early spring.

Feeding Fertilizing is generally not needed.

Problems No problems are known.

FLOWERING

Season The small pink or mauve flowers are profuse during the summer.

PRUNING

General Regular pruning is not needed. Plants may need occasional trimming. By taking regular cuttings for cooking and salads, you automatically prune the plant. Growing two or three thymes mean you can safely take plenty of leaves without massacring one plant.

TIARELLA WHERRYI
Foam flower

DELICATE TIARELLA WHERRYI *thrives here in a woodland. Its compact growth pattern also makes it ideal edging for a rock garden.*

FROTHY SPRAYS *of white flowers give* Tiarella wherryi *its pretty common name. They make a charming addition to the garden in spring.*

FEATURES

Shade or
Part Shade

Tiarella wherryi is an American clump-forming perennial, ideal for small, shady areas. Its natural habitat is shady ravines and rocky woods. The white flowers are tinged pink. The form 'Bronze Beauty' is a popular choice, with contrasting white flowers and bronze-red foliage. Good alternatives are *T. trifoliata* which makes excellent groundcover in light shade. From late spring to early summer it produces light, airy sprays of white flowers on 30cm (1ft) long panicles, held above the foliage. More invasive still is *T. cordifolia* which spreads by underground stolons.

TIARELLA AT A GLANCE

Tiarella wherryi is a North American perennial for moist, shady areas. Good show of early season flowers. Hardy to −15°C (5°F).

		RECOMMENDED VARIETIES
JAN	/	*Tiarella cordifolia*
FEB	/	*T. c.* 'Mint Chocolate'
MAR	/	*T. c.* 'Ninja'
APRIL	/	*T.* 'Elizabeth Oliver'
MAY	flowering ✽	*T. polyphylla*
JUNE	flowering ✽	*T.* 'Tiger Stripe'
JULY	foliage 🍂	*T. wherryi*
AUG	foliage 🍂	*T. wherryi* 'Bronze Beauty'
SEPT	foliage 🍂	
OCT	foliage 🍂	
NOV	/	
DEC	/	

CONDITIONS

Aspect Thrives in both dappled and darkish shade, which is its natural habitat.

Site It tolerates a wide range of soils but naturally prefers rich, fertile ground, damp but definitely not boggy.

GROWING METHOD

Propagation Division is the simplest method, though ripe seed can also be sown. Sow in pots in the autumn in a cold frame. And keep young plants well watered. Do not let them dry out.

Feeding The ground needs to be quite rich. Fork in leafmould and well-rotted organic matter in the early spring, and again in the autumn.

Problems Slugs can strike, and where this becomes a major problem treat with slug pellets. Alternatively keep patrol at night, picking them off by hand. Discard as you will.

FLOWERING

Season The flowers appear in late spring, and at the beginning of the summer.

PRUNING

General Not necessary, but with more invasive kinds prune in the growing season when growth threatens to get out of control.

VERONICA
Speedwell

GENEROUS VERONICAS *bear masses of rather stately spires in summer, making them invaluable plants for the front of a border.*

THE GENTLE POWDER-BLUE blooms of Veronica gentianoides *can be used effectively to offset the brighter colours of other flowers.*

FEATURES

Full Sun

Veronicas are sun-loving plants, and include annuals, perennials and sub-shrubs. *Veronica gentianoides* comes from the Caucasus and is a mat-forming perennial with shiny leaves and spires of pale blue flowers that open in early summer. Growing 45cm (18in) high and wide, it is good in a border. 'Variegata' has creamier leaves than the species, *V. spicata* 'Icicle' has white flowers and *V. peduncularis* 'Georgia Blue' dark blue flowers. If you need a low-growing plant that spreads well, try *V. prostrata*. It grows 15cm (6in) high, and has a spread of 40cm (16in).

VERONICA AT A GLANCE

Veronica gentianoides provides a fine array of pale blue flowers in early summer, cooling down hotter adjacent colours. Hardy to –15°C (5°F).

JAN	/	RECOMMENDED VARIETIES
FEB	/	*Veronica austriaca* 'Shirley
MAR	/	Blue'
APRIL	foliage 🌿	*V. cinerea*
MAY	foliage 🌿	*V. gentianoides*
JUNE	flowering ❀	*V. g.* 'Variegata'
JULY	foliage 🌿	*V. peduncularis* 'Georgia Blue'
AUG	foliage 🌿	*V. prostrata*
SEPT	foliage 🌿	*V. spicata* 'Icicle'
OCT	foliage 🌿	*V. s.* 'Rotfuchs'
NOV	/	*V. s.* 'Wendy'
DEC	/	

CONDITIONS

Aspect   Only grow in full sunlight. *V. gentianoides* needs wall-to-wall sun and will not tolerate anything less than this.

Site   The key to success is very good drainage. The soil need not be that fertile, and in fact can be quite poor. South-facing banks or slopes often make a very good site.

GROWING METHOD

Propagation   Since veronica does not provide the fastest kind of groundcover, it is well worth propagating several more plants. Either divide them in the spring or in the autumn, or sow plenty of seed in the autumn.

Feeding   Not necessary, but in poor, unpampered soil add a slow-release fertilizer in the spring.

Problems   The main problem is usually downy mildew, which is best tackled by quickly removing all affected leaves, thus providing better air circulation around the plant. Powdery mildew needs to be tackled with a chemical spray.

FLOWERING

Season   *V. gentianoides* gives a good but brief show of flowers in early summer.

PRUNING

General   Pruning is not necessary.

VINCA MINOR
Periwinkle

NEATLY EDGED in cream, the foliage of this variegated periwinkle is very decorative. The plant has a dense growth habit.

PERIWINKLE CARPETS an extensive area in this garden and contrasts well with the dwarf sacred bamboo and dark laurustinus.

FEATURES

Sun or Part Shade

Vinca minor comes in a plain green-leaved form and several variegated forms, including 'Argenteovariegata', although the blue flowers are, as a rule, more profuse on the plain form. They appear during the spring. The plant has a creeping growth habit, rooting down at the nodes, and one plant will eventually cover 1.8m (6ft). *V. minor* is an excellent carpeting plant for shaded areas under trees, on banks or in large rockeries. Its growth can be rather vigorous, even invasive in warm climates, but it is not as invasive as its close relative *V. major*, which can also be grown in gardens. *V. minor* is very easy to care for and will withstand poor conditions, although growth will be more attractive if it is given some care.

VINCA AT A GLANCE

V. minor never fails. Masses of groundcover and a long season with blue flowers. Other colours are available. Hardy to −18°C (0°F).

		RECOMMENDED VARIETIES
JAN	foliage	*Vinca major*
FEB	foliage	
MAR	foliage	*V. m.* 'Maculata'
APRIL	foliage	*V. m.* 'Variegata'
MAY	flowering	*V. minor*
JUNE	flowering	*V. m.* 'Argenteovariegata'
JULY	flowering	*V. m* 'Azurea Flore Pleno'
AUG	flowering	*V. m* 'Gertrude Jekyll'
SEPT	flowering	*V. m* 'Le Grave'
OCT	foliage	
NOV	foliage	
DEC	foliage	

CONDITIONS

Aspect   *V. minor* grows best in shade, in filtered sunlight or with morning sun and afternoon shade. However, the greater the amount of sunshine received, the more the plant will flower over a longer period.

Site   Tolerates any kind of soil but prefers a well-drained soil enriched with organic matter.

GROWING METHOD

Propagation   Layering is the easiest way to produce more plants. Rooted sections can also be dug up, or semi-ripe cuttings can be taken in the summer. Given the rate at which it produces, you are unlikely to need to propagate more plants once the earmarked site has been well planted with *V. minor*.

Feeding   Apply complete plant food once new growth begins in spring.

Problems   No specific problems are known.

FLOWERING

Season   The mauve-blue flowers of *V. minor* appear in spring. Note that there are also many different forms which have plum or purple, pale blue and white flowers.

Cutting   Flowers are not suitable for cutting.

PRUNING

General   May need occasional pruning to control its shape and spread. If it gets out of hand you can be as ruthless as you like.

VIOLA HEDERACEA
Ivy-leaved violet

THE DELICATE FLOWERS *of ivy-leaved violet have great appeal as they push their way up through the mass of bright leaves.*

IVY-LEAVED VIOLET *forms a thick, soft border for this pebble path and looks entirely natural as it creeps out between the stones.*

FEATURES

Shade or
Part Shade

Viola hederacea is an excellent groundcover plant that is suitable for shaded and semi-shaded positions. It is easy to maintain, but can be rather invasive where the conditions are suitable. *V. hederacea* is best kept out of rockeries as it can be almost impossible to confine it to its allotted space. The small, rounded leaves grow from 5–10cm (2–4in) high, and the pretty white and mauve violets are carried on stems above the foliage. New plantings should be spaced about 30cm (1ft) apart. This well-loved plant makes a good groundcover under trees where grass will not grow, as it will tolerate occasional foot traffic. *V. hederacea* also makes a very attractive plant for troughs and hanging baskets.

VIOLA AT A GLANCE

Viola hederacea is an evergreen violet that can cover big sweeps of ground, providing late summer flowers. Hardy to –18°C (0°F).

JAN	foliage	RECOMMENDED VARIETIES
FEB	foliage	*Viola cornuta*
MAR	foliage	*V. gracilis*
APRIL	foliage	*V. hederacea*
MAY	foliage	'Huntercombe Purple'
JUNE	foliage	*V. obliqua*
JULY	foliage	*V. odorata*
AUG	flowering	*V. sororia*
SEPT	flowering	*V.* x *wittrockiana* cultivars
OCT	foliage	
NOV	foliage	
DEC	foliage	

CONDITIONS

Aspect Dappled sunlight or shade is suitable but the flowering is better if grown in some sun.

Site Tolerates a wide range of soils, but try to avoid any extremes, either of a damp or dry kind.

GROWING METHOD

Propagation Can be readily increased from runners or by division of clumps. This is best carried out in either the spring or the autumn. Replant each section, making sure that it has got a good root system.

Feeding Feeding is generally not necessary. If the soil is extremely poor, give a light dressing of blood and bone in early spring.

Problems On the whole, *V. hederacea* is unlikely to suffer from major problems, but keep a close look out for marauding snails and slugs.

FLOWERING

Season The main flowering period is late summer. The flowers come in a wide colour range, and are either violet (light to dark) or creamy-white. If you get very close you might just be able to detect some scent.

Cutting The flowers can be cut for a miniature posy.

PRUNING

General Actual pruning is not necessary but sections may need to be pulled up or cut out if the plant is spreading where it is not wanted.

INDEX

A

Abelia spp., 14
  A. *chinesis*, A. 'Edward Goucher',
  A. *floribunda*, A. x *grandiflora*, A. x *g.*
  'Francis Mason', A. x *g.* 'Goldsport',
  A. *triflora*
Acacia spp., 15
  A. *binervia*, A. *cultriformis*,
  A. *longifolia*, A. *verticillata*
Agrostis spp., 64–5
  A. *castellana*, A. *palustris*, A. *tenuis*
Ajuga reptans, 71
  A. *r.* 'Braunherz', A. *r.* 'Burgundy
  Glow', A. *r.* 'Catlin's Giant',
  A. *r.* 'Multicolor', A. *r.* 'Tricolor',
  A. *r.* 'Variegata'
Alchemilla mollis, 72
alpine phlox, 96
Anemone spp., 73
  A. *blanda*, A. *b.* 'Radar', A. *b.* 'White
  Star', A. *hupehensis*, A. *h.*
  'Bressingham Glow', A. *h.* 'Hadspen
  Abundance', A. x *hybrida* 'Honorine
  Jobert', A. *ranunculoides*
Anthemis spp., 74
  A. 'Gralagh Gold', A. *punctata
  cupaniana*, A. *tinctoria*, A. *t.* 'Alba',
  A. *t.* 'E. C. Buxton', A. *t.* 'Kelwayi',
  A. *t.* 'Sauce Hollandaise',
  A. *t.* 'Wargrave Society'
Arabis spp., 75
  A. x *arendsii* 'Rosabella',
  A. *blepharophylla* 'Fruhlingszauber',
  A. *byroides*, A. *caucasica*, A. *c.* 'Flore
  Pleno', A. *c.* 'Variegata', A. *procurrens*
  'Variegata'
Armeria spp., 76
  A. *alliacea* 'Bees Ruby',
  A. *juniperifolia* 'Bevan's Variety',
  A. *maritima*, A. *m.* 'Bloodstone',
  A. *m.* 'Vindictive', A. *pseudarmeria*

B

baby's tears, 102
Ballota spp., 77
  B. *acetabulosa*, B. 'All Hallow's
  Green', B. *nigra*, B. *n.* 'Archer's
  Variegated', B. *pseudodictamus*
bellflower, 80
Bergenia spp., 78
  B. *Adenglut*, B. 'Baby Doll',
  B. 'Bressingham Salmon',
  B. 'Bressingham White', B. *ciliata*,
  B. *cordifolia* 'Morgenrote',
  B. *c.* 'Purpurea', B. *pupurascens*
  'Silberlicht'

C

Calluna vulgaris, 79
  C. *v.* 'Allegro', C. *v.* 'Beoley Gold',
  C. *v.* 'Blazeaway', C. *v.* 'Elsie Purnell',
  C. *v.* 'Firefly', C. *v.* 'Johnson's Blue',
  C. *v.* 'Mair's Variety', C. *v.* 'Peter
  Sparkes', C. *v.* 'Wickwar Flame'
Camellia spp., 18
  C. *japonica* 'Bob Hope', C. *j.* 'Guilio
  Nuccio', C. *j.* 'Kumasaka', C. *j.* 'Miss
  Universe', C. 'Leonard Messel',
  C. *sasanqua*, C. *s.* 'Plantation Pink',
  C. *s.* 'Narumigata', C. *s.* 'Navajo',
  C. *s.* 'Nodami-ushiro, C. x *williamsii*
  'Elsie Jury'
Campanula spp., 80
  C. 'Birch Hybrid', C. *cochleariifolia*,
  C. *garganica*, C. *glomenta*, C.
  portenschlagiana, C. *poscharskyana*,
  C. *pulla*, C. *takesimana*,
Carpinus betulus, 19
  C. *b.* 'Asplenifolia'
catmint, 93
catnip, 93
Cerastium tomentosum, 81
Chaenomeles spp., 20
  C. x *californica* 'Enchantress',
  C. *japonica*, C. *speciosa*, C. *s.*
  'Moeloosei', C. *s.* 'Simonii', C. *s.*
  'Umblicata', C. x *superba* 'Crimson
  and Gold', C. x *s.* 'Knap Hill Scarlet'
chamomile, 59
cherry laurel, 37
Chewings fescue, 65
cinquefoil, 36
comfry, 104
common beech, 28
common ivy, 70, 86
Cotoneaster spp., 21, 82
  C. *acutifolius*, 21, C. *adpressus*, 82, C.
  atropupureum, 82, C. *cashmeriensis*, 82,
  C. *conspicuus*, 21, C. *franchetti*, 21,
  C. 'Herbstfeuer', 21, 82,
  C. *horizontalis*, 21, 82, C. *hupehensis*,
  21, C. *marquandi*, 21, C. *nanshan*, 82,
  C. *nitidus*, 21, C. *perpusillus*, 82, C.
  rotundifolius, 82, C. *splendens*, 21,
  C. 'Valkenburg', 21, 82
cranesbill, 85
creeping bent, 65
creeping Jenny, 92
creeping red fescue, 64
x *Cupressocyparis leylandii*, 23
  x C. *l.* 'Castlewellan', x C. *l.* 'Galway
  Gold', x C. *l.* 'Haggerston Grey',
  x C. *l.* 'Harlequin', x C. *l.* 'Leighton
  House', x C. *l.* 'Naylor's Blue',
  x C. *l.* 'Robinson's Gold'
Cupressus spp., 23
  C. *abramsiana*, C. *bakeri*, C. *goveniana*
  var. *pygmaea*, C. *macrocarpa*, C. *m.*
  'Glauca Pendula', C. *sempervirens*
  'Stricta',
cypress, 23

D

daisy bush, 34
Dianthus spp.,
  D. *armeria*, D. *a.* 'Doris', D. *deltoides*,
  D. *erinaceus* 'Haytor White, D. *e.* 'Joe
  Vernon', D. *e.* 'Mrs Sinkins',
  D. *pavonius*, D. *scardicus*, D. *superbus*

E

Elaeagnus pungens, 24
  E. *p.* 'Dicksonii', E. *p.* 'Frederici',
  E. *p.* 'Goldrim', E. *p.* 'Maculata',
  E. *p.* 'Variegata'
Elephant's ears, 78
Escallonia spp., 25
  E. *rubra* 'Crimson Spire',
  E. 'Edinensis', E. 'Peach Blossom'
Euonymus spp., 26–7
  E. *alatus*, 26, E. *cornutus* var.
  quinquecornutus, 26, E. *europaeus* 'Red
  Cascade', 26, E. *fortunei*, 26, E. *f.*
  'Emerald Gaiety', 26, E. *f.* 'Emerald
  'n' Gold', 26, E. *japonicus*, 26–7, E. *j.*
  'Aureus', 27, E. *j.* 'Macrophyllus', 27,
  E. *j.* 'Macrophyllus Aureovariegatus',
  27, E. *j.* 'Ovatus Aureus', 27,
  E. *latifolius*, 26, E. *lucidus*, 26,
  E. *planipes*, 26
Erica carnea, 84
  E. *c.* 'Adrienne Duncan', E. *c.* 'Ann
  Sparkes', E. *c.* 'Challenger', E. *c.*
  'December Red', E. *c.* 'King George',
  E. *c.* 'March Seedling', E. *c.* 'Myretoun
  Ruby', E. *c.* 'Springwood White', E. *c.*
  'Vivelli'

F

Fagus spp., 28
  Fagus sylvatica
fescue, 64
Festuca rubra var. *commutata*, 64–5
Festuca rubra var. *rubra*, 64
foam flower, 106
Fuchsia spp., 29
  F. *magellanica*, F. 'Mrs Popple',
  F. 'Riccartonii'

G

golden privet, 32
Geranium spp., 85
  G. 'Anne Folkard', G. *endressii*, G.
  himalayense 'Gravetye', G. 'Johnson's
  Blue', G. x *oxonianum* 'Wargrave
  Pink', G. *pratense* 'Mrs Kendall Clark',
  G. *psilostemon*, G. *sylvaticum*
  'Mayflower'

Published by Murdoch Books UK Ltd, 2001
Ferry House, 51–57 Lacy Road, Putney, London SW15 1PR

ISBN 1 85391 848 2

A catalogue of this book is available from the British Library.

SERIES EDITOR: Graham Strong

COMMISSIONING EDITOR: Iain MacGregor

EDITOR: Richard Rosenfeld

PROJECT EDITOR: Angela Newton

DESK EDITOR: Alastair Laing

ILLUSTRATIONS: Sonya Naumov; Lorraine Hannay

DESIGN AND EDITORIAL: Axis Design Editions Limited

PUBLISHING MANAGER: Fia Fornari

PRODUCTION MANAGER: Lucy Byrne

PUBLISHER: Catie Ziller

CEO: Robert Oerton

GROUP CEO/PUBLISHER: Anne Wilson

GROUP GENERAL MANAGER: Mark Smith

COLOUR SEPARATION: Colourscan

Printed in China through Hanway Press

ORIGINAL TEXT: Margaret Hanks

All photographs by Lorna Rose except those by Tim Sandall (pp 1, 2, 3, 8 bottom right, 9 top right, 19, 21 right, 26 right, 41 right, 47 top, 48, 49 top, 50, 51 top, 53, 54 top, 55, 56 top, 57 top, 58 top right, 59 top right, 60, 61 top, 64, 69 top, 70 top, 78 left, 84 left, 85, 87, 88 right, 95, 103, 106); A-Z Botanical Collection (p 28); Garden Picture Library (pp 77, 100 right, 101); Photos Horticultural (p 100 left); Harry Smith Collection (pp 21 left, 24, 29, 34, 36 right, 39, 107); Merehurst © (pp 25, 26 left, 36 left, 40 left, 41 left, 47 bottom, 68, 69 bottom, 73, 78 right, 79, 84 right, 8 left, 97, 104); John Glover (p 40 right)